HEINEMANN HISTORY

THE RISE OF ISLAM

D0452587

HEINEMANN
EDUCATIONAL

John Child

503625

Heinemann Educational,
a division of Heinemann Educational Books Ltd,
Halley Court, Jordan Hill, Oxford OX2 8EJ

OXFORD LONDON EDINBURGH MADRID
ATHENS BOLOGNA PARIS MELBOURNE
SYDNEY AUCKLAND SINGAPORE TOKYO
IBADAN NAIROBI HARARE GABORONE
PORTSMOUTH NH (USA)

First published 1991

**British Library Cataloguing in Publication Data is available
from the British Library on request.**

ISBN 0–435–31277–4

Designed by Ron Kamen, Green Door Design Ltd, Basingstoke

Illustrated by Jeff Edwards

Printed in Hong Kong

The front cover shows a tile mosaic at the Mosque of Sidi
Sahab, Kairouan.

Icon information

Every Unit in this book includes the following symbol. When
a section is filled in, it indicates the availability of extra
resources included in the accompanying *Assessment and
Resources Pack*.

Unit is referred to
in an Extension
Worksheet.

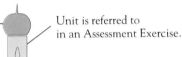

Unit is referred to
in an Assessment Exercise.

For every Unit there is a Foundation Worksheet.

Acknowledgements

The author and publisher would like to thank the following for
permission to reproduce photographs:

J. Allan Cash Ltd: 5.1E
Ancient Art & Architecture Collection: 1.2B, 2.1A,
3.1D, 3.2D
Bibliothèque Nationale: 3.5F
Bibliothèque Nationale/Islamic Foundation: 3.6B
Bollinger/Stern: 5.3D
C. M. Dixon: cover, 3.1B, 3.10B, 3.11A, 3.11C, 4.1A,
5.1A, 5.1B
Werner Forman Archive/National Museum of Anthropology,
Madrid: 3.2B
Girandon: 1.2A, 3.7D, 4.3A, 4.4B, 5.2A
Girandon/Bibliothèque National: 3.8C
Girandon/Bridgeman: 4.2B
Sonia Halliday Photographs: 1.2D, 3.3E, 3.8B, 3.9B, 3.9C,
3.10A, 3.11D, 3.12A, 4.1B, 4.2A, 4.6D, 5.1D

Robert Harding Picture Library: 1.2C, 2.5A, 3.2C,
3.7B, 3.10C, 3.12G, 4.5B
Michael Holford: 2.4A
Hutchinson Library: 3.4D, 5.1F
Islamic Foundation: 5.3C
Kobal Collection: 3.4C
The Metropolitan Museum: 3.8A
Christine Osborne: 2.5C
Picturepoint Ltd: 5.2C
Private Collection: 4.6A
Peter Sanders: 5.2B
Syndication International: 3.12F
Wayland Publishers Ltd: 3.8D
Jeremy Whitaker: 3.12H

We are also grateful to the following for permission to
reproduce copyright material:

The Muslim Educational Trust for Source 5.3B, taken from
Islam, Beliefs and Teachings by the Muslim Educational Trust,
1984.

Every effort has been made to contact copyright holders of
material reproduced in this book. Any omissions will be
rectified in subsequent printings if notice is given to the
publisher.

Thanks also to Dr Ahsan of the Islamic Foundation.

Details of written sources

In some sources the wording or sentence structure has been
simplified to ensure that the source is accessible.

M. Bianco, *Gadafi, Voice of the Desert*, Longman, 1975: 5.3A
Wilfrid Blunt, *The Splendours of Islam*, Viking Press, 1976:
3.1C, 3.11E
Hermann Bondi (Ed.), *The Rise of Islam*, Marshall Cavendish,
1969: 2.1B, 4.2C, 4.6B
R. Bruce, *Muhammad*, Holt, Rinehart and Winston, 1984:
2.2B
R. Bruce, *Islamic Worship*, Cassell, 1985: 5.1C
Trevor Cairns, *Barbarians, Christians and Muslims*, Cambridge
University Press, 1971: 2.3D
Brian Catchpole, *The Clash of Cultures*, Heinemann
Educational, 1981: 3.5E
P. W. Gardner, R. Bateman, *Core Skills in History Two*, Holmes
McDougall, 1989: 3.12B
Rosalyn Kendrick, *Islam*, Heinemann Educational, 1989: 2.2C,
2.3C, 2.4A, 2.5B, 3.5B, 3.9D
Peter Mansfield, *The Arabs*, Penguin, 1976: 2.3A
Joyce Milton, Raphael Steinberg, Sarah Lewis, *Religion at the
Crossroads*, Cassell, 1980: 4.2D, 4.3A, 4.4A, 4.6C
Malise Ruthven, *Islam in the World*, Penguin, 1984: 2.2D
Paul Shuter, John Child, David Taylor, *Skills in History*, Book
2, Heinemann Educational, 1989: 3.5D
Desmond Stewart, *Early Islam*, Time-Life Books, 1967: 3.3A,
3.3B, 3.4A, 3.5C, 3.6A
Richard Tames, *The Muslim World*, MacDonald, 1982: 3.5A
Hugh Thomas, *Spain*, Time-Life Books, 1964: 3.11B
W. Montgomery Watt, *The Majesty that was Islam*, Sidgwick
and Jackson, 1974: 2.4C, 2.5E, 3.3E
Gavin Young, *Iraq, Land of Two Rivers*, Collins, 1980: 3.3D,
3.4B

CONTENTS

1.1 The Impact of Islam (1)

Islam is one of the world's most important religions. Followers of Islam are called **Muslims.**

Islam was started in Arabia by the **Prophet Muhammad.** He was a man who lived from 570 to 632. The first Muslims were **Arabs** and they conquered nearby countries, spreading Islam amongst other people. Large parts of the world came under Arab and Muslim control.

The map below shows Muslim rule at its greatest. As the Arabs spread, taking their religion with them, they learned from the people they conquered. They wrote down what they learned in books, which were read all over the Muslim world. Then they worked to improve that knowledge. They became very advanced in art, architecture, science and mathematics. They built splendid towns like Baghdad, Damascus, Cairo and Cordoba. Many features of modern Muslim countries began then. Even countries further away, like Britain, learned a lot from the Muslims. The numbering system which we all use today came to western Europe from the Muslim world.

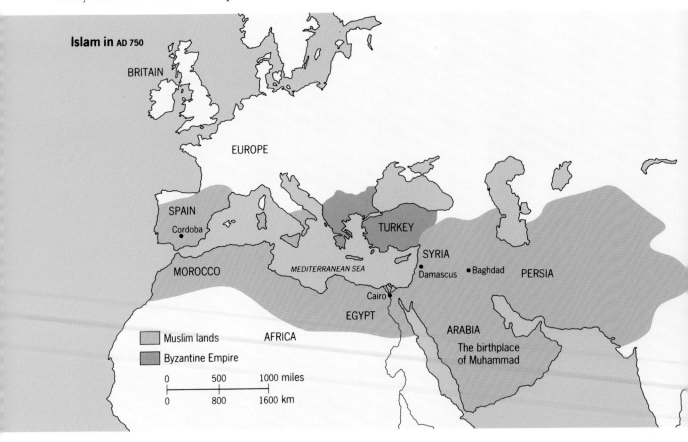

Islam in AD 750

BRITAIN

EUROPE

SPAIN
Cordoba

TURKEY

MOROCCO

MEDITERRANEAN SEA

SYRIA
Damascus •Baghdad   PERSIA

Cairo

EGYPT

ARABIA
The birthplace of Muhammad

AFRICA

☐ Muslim lands
☐ Byzantine Empire

0   500   1000 miles
0   800   1600 km

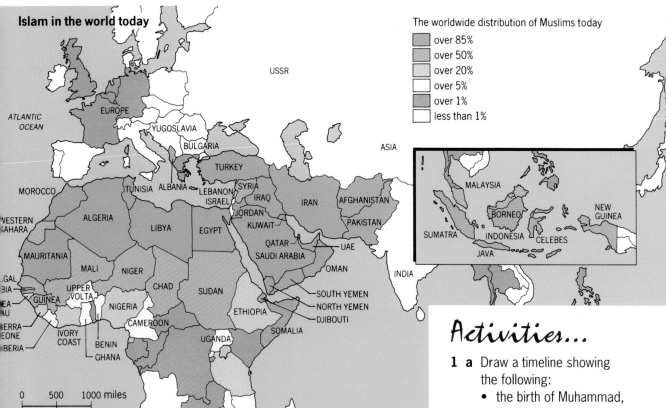

Islam in the world today

The worldwide distribution of Muslims today

- over 85%
- over 50%
- over 20%
- over 5%
- over 1%
- less than 1%

USSR

ATLANTIC OCEAN

EUROPE

YUGOSLAVIA

BULGARIA

ASIA

TURKEY

MOROCCO
TUNISIA ALBANIA
LEBANON SYRIA
ISRAEL IRAQ
JORDAN
IRAN
AFGHANISTAN

WESTERN SAHARA
ALGERIA
LIBYA
EGYPT
KUWAIT
PAKISTAN

QATAR
UAE
SAUDI ARABIA

MAURITANIA
MALI
NIGER
OMAN
INDIA

GAL
BIA
UPPER VOLTA
CHAD
SUDAN
SOUTH YEMEN
NORTH YEMEN
DJIBOUTI

EA
AU
GUINEA
NIGERIA
ETHIOPIA

IERRA EONE
IBERIA
IVORY COAST
BENIN
GHANA
CAMEROON
UGANDA
SOMALIA

MALAYSIA

BORNEO
NEW GUINEA

SUMATRA
INDONESIA
CELEBES
JAVA

| 0 | 500 | 1000 miles |
| 0 | 800 | 1600 km |

Activities...

1 a Draw a timeline showing the following:
- the birth of Muhammad,
- the death of Muhammad,
- Muslim control at its greatest,
- the Turks take control of the Muslim world,
- the Turkish Empire splits into smaller countries.

b Give your timeline a suitable title.

c Write a paragraph to explain your timeline.

2 What has been the effect of the growth of Islam on the following people:
- the people of southern Spain in the 8th century,
- the Arabs of North Africa today,
- the people of Britain today?

In each case, answer **a great effect**, **some effect**, or **no effect** and explain your answer.

Later, Arab control weakened. From about 1050 the Muslims around the Mediterranean fell under the control of new rulers, the **Turks.** They were also Muslims and spread Islam even further. At first, this was also a splendid empire, but from about 1700 the Turkish Empire became weak and started to break up. For all of this time Islam was the main religion in the area.

Eventually, in 1918, the Turkish Empire was split up into smaller countries. Saudi Arabia, Iran, Iraq and Egypt are just some of the modern Muslim countries which used to be in the Arab and Turkish Empires. They are very important countries in the modern world.

Today there are over 1,100 million Muslims. The teachings and history of Islam affect the way they think and act. Muslims are scattered throughout the world: only one sixth are Arabs and over two million Muslims live in Britain. The expansion of Islam had a huge impact on the world in the past; Islam has a vital part to play in the world today.

1.2 Sources

This book is about the way Islam grew and about the countries where the Muslims lived. It is about Muhammad, who started Islam, and his life and teaching. It is about the way the followers of Muhammad, first Arabs and then Turks, conquered huge areas of land, thus spreading the religion of Islam. It is about the towns they built over a thousand years ago, their buildings, laws, clothes, crafts, art, trade, ships, schools and medicine. It is about the battles they fought to gain and keep control of their land.

But how do we know about all of this? What is the evidence for what is written in this book?

Historians use two types of evidence: primary sources and secondary sources.

A **primary source** is evidence which comes from the time of the events being studied. We have many types of primary sources of evidence about the Islamic world. Some are **written** in Arabic, like the medical books of Arab doctors. Sometimes, travellers who went to Muslim lands would write about what they saw. Other primary sources are not written. They are called **artefacts**, things people have made. For example, some buildings survive from the time of early Muslim rule. So does some pottery, tile decorations, paintings, coins and jewellery. Weapons, clothes and carpets from one thousand years ago are very rare however.

Secondary sources are produced later by people who have studied the primary evidence and other secondary sources and come up with their own interpretations of the past. This textbook is a secondary source of evidence about the Islamic world.

A SOURCE

A medical book by a Muslim doctor showing the workings of the eye, probably 10th century.

B SOURCE

Jewelled golden helmet and mace, used by a Turkish sultan in the 16th century.

SOURCE C

The Dome of the Rock. A 7th century mosque (place of worship) built by Muslims in Jerusalem.

SOURCE D

A 16th century miniature painting showing Turkish Muslims building a castle during the time of Sultan Murad III (ruled 1574–95).

Activities...

1 How many of the sources in this unit are primary sources for the study of Islamic history between 600 and 1600? Explain your answer.

2 What do these sources tell us about:
   a how wealthy the Islamic world was?
   b how religious it was?
   c poor people in the Islamic lands?

3 What problems do you think historians have when trying to find out about Islamic history from primary sources?

2.1 Muhammad – his Early Life

Arabia was a very poor area, mostly desert or scrub. Many Arabs made a living from tending sheep. Some of these were **bedouins** who were nomads, constantly moving their sheep, camels and tents from place to place. Others used camels in groups, called **caravans**, to carry goods from town to town to sell. The Arabs were split into many tribes. There was no single king who ruled them. They had no single religion either. Most Arabs worshipped several gods and spirits that they believed lived in rocks and trees.

Muhammad was born in 570 in **Mecca*** (Makkah), a trading town on the caravan routes. It had the country's most sacred temple, a cube shaped building called the **Ka'ba**. The Ka'ba had over 360 altars, statues and other religious objects or idols which the Arabs worshipped. People travelled many miles to worship there.

Muhammad belonged to an important tribe, the **Koraish**, (Quraysh). They charged fees to all the traders and worshippers who came to Mecca. But Muhammad was an orphan by the age of six and quite poor. He worked on the caravans. He disliked life in Mecca. There was too much fighting and greed among the tribes; women, children and the poor were badly treated; there was too much drunkenness and gambling; people worshipped all kinds of idols. From about 610 Muhammad spent more time alone, thinking and praying on nearby Mount Hira. Then he started to get messages from God. Muhammad told his friends about the messages. He called them **revelations**; truths revealed to him by God. Straight away some people wrote them down. Eventually they were collected together in a book called the **Koran** (Qur'an).

In the revelations, an angel said that Muhammad was the last of God's prophets (messengers) and more important than those before, like Jesus. Muhammad began to preach these messages to the people. He said there was only one God (the Arabic for God is **Allah**); that it was evil to worship idols; that greed was wrong; that Allah would judge everyone when they died and send them to Heaven or Hell; that God's followers should obey Him before all others. Islam means submission (to God's will).

Arabia at the time of the birth of Muhammad

BYZANTINE EMPIRE

PERSIA

MEDITERRANEAN SEA

Damascus

Cairo

Baghdad

miles
0   250   500
0   400   800
km

Medina

PERSIAN GULF

Mecca

ARABIA

RED SEA

INDIAN OCEAN

—— Major trade routes

Muhammad gained many followers, especially among the poor. But Islam was not popular with the rich in Mecca. They feared losing their money, their religions and their power. In 622 many Muslims began to move away from Mecca to settle in **Medina** (Madinah), a nearby town. In Medina, the Muslims were welcomed. Eventually, Muhammad also left for Medina, chased by the Koraish. They offered a prize of 100 camels for his capture. This move to Medina is called the **hijrah**.

The birth of Christ is so important to Christians that they count their dates from then. The hijrah is so important to Muslims that they start counting their history from then. So the year AD 622 is the year 1 AH (After Hijrah) for Muslims.

*Note about spelling
The Arabs use a different alphabet from ours (see Source A). We can only write Arabic words in English by writing something that sounds right. There are no agreed English spellings. For Muhammad, you may see Mohammed or Mohammad; for Mecca, Makkah; for Koran, Qur'an. In this book we have used the spellings most familiar in English. Other spellings are given once in brackets. Sometimes Muslims prefer the other spellings.

B

SOURCE

At the dead of night, soldiers burst into the house. They were sent to arrest him as an enemy of the people and a danger to the city. But Muhammad and his friend Abu Bakr slipped away into the desert hills where they hid in a cave.

A *modern historian writing in 'The Rise of Islam', 1969.*

Activities...

1 What changes did Muhammad want to see in the lives of the people of Mecca?

2 'The Koraish hated Muhammad because they feared losing their money, their religions and their power.'
   a Explain this statement.
   b Does Source B agree with the statement?

3 Historians use documents as sources. What can the Koran tell historians?

A

SOURCE

The Koran is the Muslim book of God's revelations to Muhammad. It is always read aloud in Arabic.

2.2 Muhammad – his Later Life

Muhammad arrived in Medina with several of his followers. The people there welcomed him as the prophet of God and found places in their homes for the Muslims. Muhammad continued to preach and got more followers. He soon became the leader of Medina. People looked to him to solve disputes in the town and with other tribes. He started to arrange collections for the needy. Gradually, he began to make laws for people to follow, including rules about marriage, divorce and food. He was still getting messages from God and these were more and more about how people should lead their lives. For example, Chapter 17 of the Koran includes commands for Muslims to be kind to their parents and the old and to be generous. Islam gave status and the hope of Heaven to the poor; Muhammad's laws brought justice and order. Medina had become a small Islamic state with Muhammad as its leader.

B **SOURCE**

Permission is given by God to those who are fighting because they have been wronged, they have been driven from their homes for no reason.

The Koran, Chapter 22 (verse 40).

C **SOURCE**

The Meccans were still determined to harm Muhammad. They tried to bribe the Medinans to hand him over. They persecuted the relatives of the Muslims in Mecca. In 623 a small group of Muslims raided a camel train. Although Muhammad had not planned this attack, he understood their reasons. Sadly it provided the Meccans with an excuse to attack Medina with a full army. Muhammad only had 313 warriors, including young boys. They marched out of the city, determined to die for God if they must. To everyone's amazement, their faith and courage won the day.

From 'Islam' by Rosalyn Kendrick, 1989.

A **SOURCE**

A painting of the Battle of Badr, painted many years after the event.

A huge force of nearly 1,000 men was sent by the Koraish to escort the next caravan. They then advanced upon Medina. Muhammad chose to make his stand at the water wells of Badr. He had three of the four wells filled in. The tired and thirsty Meccans had to fight for water on ground chosen by their enemies.

From 'Islam in the World', by Malise Ruthven, 1984.

But tension between the Muslims and the Koraish in Mecca continued. The Meccans accused the Muslims of raiding their trade caravans. In 624, the Meccans sent an army of about 1,000 men to punish the Muslims. The Muslims only had a force of 300 but they were very loyal and brave. They won the fight, called the **Battle of Badr**. The Muslims were now a fighting force as well as a religious group. Muhammad made treaties with other Arab tribes to make sure that they didn't join the Meccans. Some of these tribes became Muslims.

Fighting continued for the next few years. Muhammad sometimes led the Muslims in battle; once he was wounded in the face and leg. He was a successful general. Eventually, the Muslims wore down the Meccans and in 630 Muhammad took his followers back to Mecca in triumph. He went directly to the Ka'ba, took out all of the altars and idols and declared it a temple to Allah alone. This was a wise decision since the Ka'ba was known all over Arabia and it became a place of worship for all Muslims. By a mixture of preaching, persuasion and force, the Muslims soon controlled all of the main tribes and towns of Arabia.

Muhammad became ill in 632 and died. In about 23 years he had started a religion which had come to dominate the lives of thousands of followers and was still expanding.

Activities...

1 **a** What did Muhammad do to help the growth of Islam as:
   i a preacher?
   ii a soldier?
   iii a wise leader?

 b How much was the growth of Islam due to:
   i people finding God's messages attractive?
   ii Muhammad's loyal followers?

 c How far do you think the success of Islam was due to one man, Muhammad?

2 Read Source C. It was written by a Muslim. Compared to some other accounts, it is quite kind to the Muslims and harsh towards the Meccans.
 a Can you find any examples of this?
 b Does this make the source wrong?
 c If Source C **were** wrong, would it still be useful to a historian?

3 **a** If historians wanted to find out why the Muslims were successful in battle, what help could they get from Sources A, B, C and D?
 b Which do you think is the most useful source?

2.3 Arab Expansion

When Muhammad died, Muslims controlled most of Arabia. Soon they started expanding much further. Why did they do this?

Some Arabs were eager to spread Islam. The Koran promised that any Muslim who died in battle for his religion would go to Heaven. It also said that Allah supported the use of war to defend Muslims against enemies of Islam. Others joined the attacks for the riches they brought. They wanted to expand into the fertile land of the Persian Empire and the Byzantine Empire (the remains of the Roman Empire).

The success of the Arabs was amazing. By 640, moving north, they had captured Jerusalem and Damascus and controlled Syria. Soon after, they conquered Persia. Arab armies also headed west. By 642 these armies captured Cairo and took control of Egypt. A navy was created and Cyprus was captured in 649. By 670 the Arabs had occupied Tunisia and in 708 they reached the Atlantic Ocean. Striking east, they had reached Samarkand by 676 and the borders of India by 707. Victory at the **Battle of Talas** in 751 against the Chinese secured central Asia. From such a humble start, how had they done it? The sources in this unit give some clues.

A **SOURCE**

The Arab tactics were simple. They would charge the enemy and cast a shower of javelins. They would repeat this until the enemy showed signs of breaking and then start hand to hand combat. They were usually outnumbered and the superiority of their enemies should have been overwhelming. The Arabs had no siege equipment (to help them break down the defences of a city or fortress).

From 'The Arabs' by Peter Mansfield, 1976.

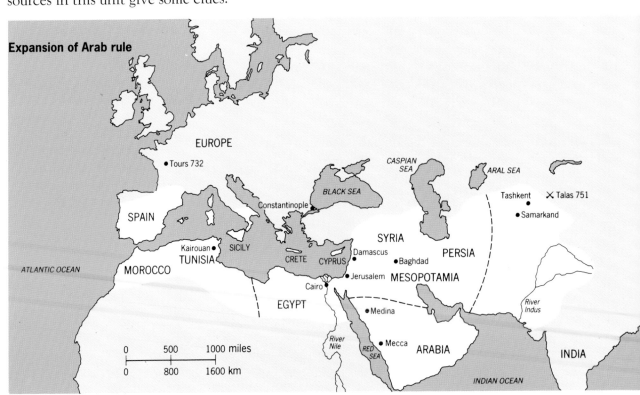

Expansion of Arab rule

EUROPE

• Tours 732

CASPIAN SEA

ARAL SEA

BLACK SEA

Tashkent • ✕ Talas 751

• Samarkand

SPAIN

Constantinople •

SYRIA

Kairouan • SICILY

TUNISIA

CRETE

CYPRUS

Damascus •

PERSIA

• Baghdad

ATLANTIC OCEAN

MOROCCO

• Jerusalem

MESOPOTAMIA

Cairo •

EGYPT

River Indus

• Medina

River Nile

RED SEA

• Mecca

ARABIA

INDIA

INDIAN OCEAN

0 500 1000 miles
0 800 1600 km

B

SOURCE

A 10th century bowl from Mesopotamia. It may give us some clues about the weapons of the Muslim soldiers.

C

SOURCE

There were many reasons for this rapid expansion:

- there was white-hot enthusiasm amongst the Muslims. Muhammad inspired great devotion in his people.
- the new faith was vastly superior to the old idol worship of Arabia; this was obvious to any thinking person.
- many Jews and Christians found Islam a more logical and reasonable belief.
- Persia and Byzantium were both weak during this period, having fought each other for some 200 years.
- the ideal Muslim fought with courage and compassion.

From 'Islam' by Rosalyn Kendrick, 1989.

D

SOURCE

Within a few years, they had destroyed the Persian Empire, which had already been weakened by the Byzantines. Against the Byzantines, their task was easier because the people were tired of heavy taxes. They had been persecuted because of differences of opinion about some points of the Christian religion. They expected better treatment from the Muslims. In North Africa the fierce Berbers became Muslims and added new strength to the Arab armies.

The Arabs were tough men. They knew that if they were killed in this holy war, Allah would reward them in paradise. They believed that Allah had decided that Islam would triumph.

From 'Barbarians, Christians and Muslims' by Trevor Cairns, 1971.

Activities...

1 a Copy the map on page 12. Find a way of showing how Arab rule spread over time.

b People's reasons for doing things are called their **motives**. What were the motives behind the Arab expansion?

2 Sources A–D give us clues about why the Arab armies were so successful.

a Make a list of as many reasons as you can find.

b Do all of the sources give all of the same reasons? Why do you think this is?

c Source C is written by a Muslim. Do you think that this influences the reasons given?

3 Sources can sometimes tell us things indirectly. Source A does not mention religion. Yet it may tell us something about the religious beliefs of the Arabs. How?

2.4 The Rightly-Guided Caliphs

After Muhammad died, in 632, the Muslims needed a new leader – for their country and for Islam, their religion. It was not clear who should take over from Muhammed as leader of the Muslims. A group of Muhammad's closest friends chose Abu Bakr to be their new leader. The Muslims gave him the title of **caliph**, which means successor or deputy. As caliph, Abu Bakr was ruler of the new Muslim territories and defender of the Islamic religion. Abu Bakr was succeeded by three other caliphs – Umar, Uthman and Ali. The first four leaders followed Muhammad's example closely. Like him, they used the rules of Islam to govern the Muslims. They lived simple lives and tried to rule fairly. But their rule was also a time when the Muslims were constantly fighting to make Islam stronger. They encouraged wars and battles against other Arabs and against outsiders, saying they were necessary to remove injustice and the enemies of Islam.

Arabs swearing allegiance to Caliph Ali after the murder of Caliph Uthman. (A painting produced many years after the event.)

B

SOURCE

During the 30 years after 632, the Muslims were governed by four **caliphs**, who were outstanding men chosen for their good character. They were unselfish and tolerant, knew the Koran, and had been Muhammad's dearest friends. The word caliph means successor. These first four caliphs were known as the 'rightly-guided' caliphs because they followed Muhammad's example closely.

Abu Bakr ruled for only two years. He was followed by **Umar**, a giant of a man, from 634–44. When he went to Jerusalem, he set out with only one servant and a camel, which he and the servant took turns to ride. Umar lived all his life without luxuries.

Uthman then became the leader. He was a simple and kind-hearted man. But he angered the people of Egypt by replacing the governor with his own cousin, who set higher taxes. A group of Egyptians killed Uthman in 656.

Ali, the next caliph, was opposed by many Muslims including Uthman's cousin Muawiya. There was constant argument. In 661 Ali was also struck down while at prayer in the mosque. He did not die for three days, during which time he protected and fed his assassin.

From 'Islam' by Rosalyn Kendrick, 1989.

C

SOURCE

At Muhammad's death the gentle, faithful but aged Abu Bakr was appointed caliph. His commanders, with his blessing, set out on a jihad (holy war) against Syria.

Abu Bakr died after reigning only two years. He was followed by the bad-tempered Umar (634–644) then the aged and incompetent Uthman (644–656). Both of these men were killed by angry subjects.

Ali, son-in-law of Muhammad, became the fourth caliph (656–661). But some Muslims wouldn't accept him. Ali spent his entire five-year reign in internal warfare. One of his enemies was Ayesha, Muhammad's widow. In 656, at the Battle of Basra, she was taken prisoner on a battlefield strewn with 13,000 corpses. Ali, always merciful, kept her safe but under guard where she could do him no harm. In 661 he too was killed by an assassin.

Adapted from the work of a modern historian writing in 'The Rise of Islam', 1969. It is interesting that Muslim accounts of the battle at Basra put the number of deaths at about 6,000.

Activities...

1 **a** Draw a timeline to show how long each of the four 'rightly-guided' caliphs ruled.

b In what ways did the 'rightly-guided' caliphs carry on the example of Muhammad?

2 **a** Read Source B. On a piece of rough paper, make a tick every time it says something nice about the four caliphs, a cross for everything bad about them, and a small circle for everything which is not good or bad, just information. Then do the same for Source C. Compare the ticks, crosses and circles. What do they tell you about the two sources?

b To learn about these caliphs, would you:
  i use only Source B?
  ii use only Source C?
  iii believe everything in both sources?
  iv use both sources carefully?
  Explain your answer.

3 Finish this sentence. 'Sources A, B and C are secondary sources of evidence about the caliphs because ...'

2.5 Sunni and Shi'ites

The last unit told how the Muslims argued about who should be the caliph. Some supported **Ali.** Ali was Muhammad's closest living relative. He was his cousin and married to his youngest daughter, Fatima. Other Muslims supported **Muawiya,** Uthman's cousin. Muawiya was one of the powerful **Umayyad** family. They were part of the Koraish tribe who first opposed Muhammad. Many of them had only become Muslims just before Muhammad died. Muawiya's supporters said that it was wrong for the leadership of Islam to stay in Muhammad's family. They said that the most able Muslim should be the leader. He should rule by using the Koran and Muhammad's ways (Sunnah). These Muslims were called the **Sunni.**

Ali's supporters said that Muhammad's family should succeed him and that he had trained Ali as his successor. They didn't accept that Abu Bakr, Umar and Uthman had been real caliphs. Some of them cursed them in their chants. They thought that Muawiya and his followers were half-hearted Muslims, more interested in power than Islam. Ali's supporters were called the **Shia Ali** (party of Ali), or **Shi'ites** for short.

When Ali died, his son Husain tried to get the caliphate back for his family. But he was killed in battle and became a Shi'ite **martyr.** (See Source B.)

Shi'ite Muslims at prayer in present-day Iran.

A SOURCE

B SOURCE

In 681, Husain and about 70 men were surrounded at Karbala by an army of 4,000 supporters of Yazid, Muawiya's son. They were close to water but Yazid's army denied them drink. For eight days, they tried to get Husain to give up his claim to be the next caliph, but he refused.

Outnumbered, his followers were killed. When Husain held out his baby son for mercy, an arrow, fired through the baby's neck, pinned him to Husain's arm. At the end, the body of Husain, riddled with arrows, was trampled in the mud. His head was hacked off and taken back to Yazid.

The shrine where Husain was buried at Karbala became a holy place for Shi'ites. They worship there every year and weep for the victory of evil over good. They promise to defend their beliefs as Husain did.

From 'Islam' by Rosalyn Kendrick, 1989.

The Shi'ites never regained control of Islam. There were always many more Sunni. Today, about ten per cent of Muslims are Shi'ites. But they are a powerful minority. Iran is ruled by Shi'ites. Many more Shi'ites live in Pakistan and Iraq. They believe that one day the final successor to Ali, called the **Mahdi**, will come to set up the perfect Muslim state.

Activities...

1 a Explain Ali's claim to lead Islam.
   b Explain Muawiya's claim.

2 Read Source B. How do you think Muslim readers would respond to this account today?

3 Muslims remember Ali as a true Muslim. Some Muslims think Muawiya was more interested in power.
   a Do Sources D and E support this view?
   b Do they prove this view?

4 How can you tell from this unit that the Shi'ites have stayed strong since the days of Ali?

SOURCE D

Sayings of Ali:

- If you love Allah, reject your heart's love of the world.
- One who is proud of worldly possessions in life is ignorant.

SOURCE E

I have come to you with the authority of God to rule you. It is your duty to obey me in what I think is best. It is your right that I should be fair. If you see me managing your affairs well, respond to me well.

Muawiya, quoted in 'The Majesty that was Islam' by W. Montgomery Watt, 1974.

SOURCE C

A Shi'ite mosque, near Baghdad in present-day Iraq. It was built in the 16th century.

3.1 The Umayyads

Even before Ali died, Muawiya claimed to be the true caliph. His family, the **Umayyads**, provided the next fourteen caliphs. They ruled until 750. Muawiya moved the capital of Islam from the holy city of Medina to **Damascus,** capital of **Syria.** He had been governor of Syria for Uthman. His supporters and his army were there. Each Umayyad caliph named a relative to be his successor before he died. This was to avoid arguments. But it meant that a ruling family was being created.

The Umayyads ruled well for a while. Under them, Arab rule grew to the borders of modern-day France in the west and India in the east. They built fabulous mosques like the **Dome of the Rock** in Jerusalem (see page 7). They allowed their people to bring their problems to them and consulted advisers about their policies. They were just like the Arab sheiks of the desert. They kept many of the efficient Christian clerks of the Byzantine Empire, but put Arabs in the top jobs. They had a postal system using riders on horseback to reach all parts of their lands. Arabic replaced Greek and Persian as the language of the captured territory. They started the first Arab coinage, the gold **dinar** and the silver **dirham.** Before this, the Arabs had used the coins of other countries. All of this meant the Umayyads had firmer control than any caliphs before.

But they started to neglect the rules of Islam. They did not base their laws on the Koran. They were not good Muslims like earlier caliphs. They built lavish palaces outside the towns, where they spent their time hunting or drinking and dancing, surrounded by beautiful women, poets and musicians. Their subjects became unhappy with the Umayyads.
Many Muslims, especially the Shi'ites, thought that the beliefs

A silver dirham minted by the Umayyads in the 7th century. It shows the governor of a captured territory.

A SOURCE

The court is paved with white marble. The walls of the mosque are faced with multi-coloured marble and above this are mosaics of gold and other colours, showing figures of trees and towns and beautiful inscriptions. Every well known tree and town can be found on these walls. The capitals of the columns are covered with gold, and the vaulting above is decorated with mosaic in arabesque designs.

A 10th century visitor describing the court of the Great Mosque at Damascus, built between 705 and 715.

C SOURCE

Handsome and enormously strong, a poet and musician, Walid II led the good life at his palace at Mshatta, where he filled his swimming pool with wine, and missed public prayers when he was not in a mood, or a condition, to appear. He was murdered in 744.

From 'The Splendors of Islam' by Wilfrid Blunt, 1976.

of Islam were being forgotten. The Christians and Jews under Arab control became restless too. They didn't like having to pay more taxes than Muslims. The Persians were also restless. They had a glorious history and didn't like the way the Arabs looked down upon them. The bedouin soldiers, who had fought for the land the Umayyads ruled, began to settle down and live as farmers. Many of them didn't want to fight for the Umayyads any longer.

A group of Arabs began to use this discontent to stir up trouble against the Umayyads. They had settled in the lands captured from the Persian Empire but they were Arab descendants of one of Muhammad's uncles, al-Abbas. They called themselves the **Abbasids.** They started a propaganda campaign against the Umayyads. Then they raised an army from their supporters. At the **Battle of the Great Zab** in 750, they defeated and killed the caliph. Umayyad control of Islam thus ended.

Mosaics, pictures made up of tiny pieces of tile, around the arches and columns of the Great Mosque at Damascus, 715.

Activities...

1 Compare Islam under the 'rightly-guided' caliphs with Islam under the Umayyads. What had changed? What had not?

2 The Abbasids mounted a propaganda campaign against the Umayyads. Think about the complaints people had about the Umayyads. Write a speech for an Abbasid supporter trying to get support for the Abbasid uprising.

3 a For historians studying the Umayyad Empire, which of the sources in this unit are primary sources? Which are artefacts and which are documentary sources?
   b List five other things which could be used as primary sources.

D

SOURCE

3.2 Early Islamic Art

Before Muhammad, the Arabs were mostly nomadic farmers or traders. They had little art of their own. But as Arab rule expanded, they settled down among Greeks and Syrians in the north, Persians in the east and Egyptians and Berbers in the west. They therefore 'discovered' the art of all these people. As they built their new towns, mosques and palaces, they used the best local craftsmen to help them. But the Arabs didn't just take the art of other people. They influenced the work they had done. So a new, typically Islamic, style of art arose. It can be seen in the years 600–1000 all around the Muslim world – local styles with a clear Arab influence.

For example, the Arabs learned about **mosaics** from the Byzantines. These are pictures on walls or floors made of small pieces of tile, stone or glass. The Dome of the Rock in Jerusalem and the Great Mosque in Damascus have large mosaics. Following Arab tastes, scenes from nature are common. But so are shapes and **patterns**. The Arabs liked work in **stucco**, fine plaster to decorate walls and columns. Patterns can also be seen in **window grills**, carved from stone or marble or made of metal. Early Muslims also made patterns on gold and silver and on ornaments carved from ivory, wood and rock crystal. The most famous pattern is called **arabesque** (a design of flowing lines, often with leaves and flowers). There were probably many **wall paintings** in the Umayyad mosques and palaces. But there is a problem with these. Many early mosques and palaces were made from brick, not stone. Brick is soft and does not last well. Some buildings were also destroyed later by invaders.

The Arabs also developed new ways of decorating **pottery**. One was a new shiny look called **lustreware**, which was also used on **tiles**. There were also splendid **carpets**, sometimes woven from silk. But no carpets survive from this period. Everyday articles such as pots and carpets were used and thrown away by their owners. They didn't make an effort to save them for us!

Early Arabic writing, known as **Kufic**, looks very simple. But the Koran was written in Arabic. So Muslims developed more and more attractive forms of writing, until it became an art form. This art of beautiful writing is called **calligraphy** and can be seen on Islamic books, paintings, pottery, mosaics and carpets. It is the most common feature of Islamic art.

SOURCE

A bowl decorated with kufic script, made in eastern Iran in the 10th century. The inscription says, 'Generosity is characteristic of the people of paradise'.

B

SOURCE

An ivory casket from Spain made in about 1050. It is typical of Muslim work and has calligraphic decoration round the rim.

C

SOURCE

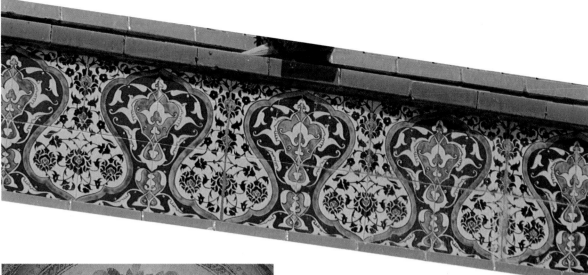

Tile decorations from the Dome of the Rock mosque, Jerusalem, built in the 7th century.

D

SOURCE

A mosaic floor from the bath of an Umayyad palace built in about 740.

E

SOURCE

A 10th century dish made in eastern Iran. The pattern was made by painting the design and then covering it with a transparent glaze.

Activities...

1 Explain each of the following:
   a mosaic,   **b** stucco,
   c lustreware,   **d** calligraphy.

2 **a** Why might the desert lifestyle of the Arabs described on pages 8–9 have discouraged Islamic art?
   b Why might the lifestyle of the Umayyad caliphs described on pages 18–19 have encouraged Islamic art?

3 Use the sources and the text in this unit to describe the special features of early Islamic art.

4 Why is it difficult for historians to get a full and accurate picture of early Islamic art?

5 What other sources would you like to be able to see in order to find out more about early Islamic art?

3.3 The Abbasids

We saw in Unit 3.1 how the **Umayyads**, who ruled the Islamic world from Damascus until 750, were overthrown by the Abbasids. But more changed than just the ruling family.

The **Abbasids** were Arabs who were descended from Muhammad's family. But they had settled in the area captured from the Persian Empire and intermarried with Persians. They adopted Persian customs and employed Persian officials. They shut themselves away behind the walls of their palaces and lived lives of glorious luxury, like the old Persian kings. They even started to claim holy status, calling themselves 'The Shadow of God on Earth'. Even Muhammad had not gone this far. The 'rightly-guided' caliphs had mixed with their people and lived fairly ordinary lives. The Umayyads had consulted with other Arab sheiks and taken advice from them. The old Arab ways were changing.

The Abbasids also built a new capital at **Baghdad**. It became a centre for world trade. Ships came to Baghdad along the River Tigris or the River Euphrates:
- from China, bringing silk, ink and peacocks,
- from India with rubies, silver, ebony and dyes,
- from Egypt with grain and glass,
- from Africa with slaves and gold,
- from Spain with leather,
- from Russia with furs.

The Muslim traders also brought back knowledge, ideas and skills from the countries they visited. For example, the Arabs learned how to make paper from the Chinese in about 750. The Islamic world became a mixture of cultures: Arab, Persian and others from all over the world. The early years of the Abbasid era were the richest period of Islamic history.

The Abbasid dynasty at Baghdad lasted 500 years, until 1258. Many things changed in the Islamic world during this time and we shall see in later units how the Abbasids lost control of their lands. But some things did not change. The borders of Islam stayed the same, stretching from India and China in the east to the Atlantic Ocean in the west. Arabic remained the common language and laws were still based on the Koran. Islam, founded by the Arabs, remained unchallenged as the religion.

Caliph Abu Jafar adopted the name of al-Mansur. It means 'the one helped to victory by God' and was chosen to make it seem that the ruler was supported by God. Harun's title was al-Rashid, 'the rightly-guided'.

From 'The Majesty that was Islam' by W. Montgomery Watt, 1974.

Consider Caliph Harun's titles : 'The Holy, the Just, the High-Born, the Omnipotent; the Gardener of the Vale of Islam, the Lion of the Impassable Forests, the Rider of the Spotless Horse, the Cypress on the Golden Hill, the Master of Spears, the Shadow of God on Earth, the Commander of the Faithful... The Caliph!'

From 'Iraq, Land of Two Rivers' by Gavin Young, 1980.

Activities...

1 Compare the Abbasids with the Umayyads:
  a What remained the same?
  b What changed?

2 How could the caliphs' titles help them to stay in control of their people?

3 Make a list of the things Source E can tell us about the Islamic world under the Abbasids. How many things has your class listed?

A miniature painting dated 1237. It shows the caliph's standard bearers announcing his arrival.

3.4 Baghdad

Abu Jafar al-Mansur, the second Abbasid caliph, built a new capital in 762. He chose a trading village called **Baghdad**. It was on the banks of the River Tigris and linked to the River Euphrates by canal. It took four years to build. Under the caliph **Harun al-Rashid** (786–809), it was the most splendid city in the world. We have Arabic manuscripts and travellers' accounts which describe it. Baghdad had 1.5 million people, measured five miles across and had hundreds of mosques and over 65,000 public baths. It had gardens, racetracks and pavilions. Many people who lived there gave up some of their Arab ways of the desert, using mattresses and tables, adopting porcelain from the Chinese, and developing the games of polo, backgammon and chess from the East.

Poetry and literature also blossomed in Baghdad. The book *Tales of the Arabian Nights* dates from this time. It is a collection of stories from all over the world. Some are set in Baghdad and feature Harun and his family. These include the stories of Aladin, Ali Baba, Sinbad the Sailor and the beautiful princess Scheherazade. They paint a fairy-story world of dashing Arab princes riding pure white horses through a city of bustling market places and sparkling minarets. It is a picture repeated in countless films. It is based on the truth, but it gives us a distorted view of what things were really like.

B SOURCE

I slipped back into my dream as we flew into Iraq, a dream of Baghdad formed by two old Hollywood movies, *The Thief of Baghdad*, and *A Thousand and One Nights*. In it, I float in a gleaming technicolour city of towering walls and arched gates, golden domes and minarets like sticks of candy. Harun al-Rashid, surrounded by slaves bearing scimitars, sits there and a beautiful girl in see-through Oriental trousers belly-dances to the sound of tambourines, flutes, harps and – strangely – jazz saxophones.

From 'Iraq, Land of Two Rivers' by Gavin Young, 1980.

A SOURCE

Baghdad was built in the form of a circle nearly two miles across with a deep moat surrounding three huge, sloping walls. Of these, the middle one was the largest, some 112 feet in height, 164 feet wide at the base and 46 feet across the top. It was fortified with look-out towers. The round city was cut into four wedge-shaped parts by two highways which cut across it at right angles, with gates through each of the walls. The space between the middle and outer walls was left clear for defence. Between the middle and inner walls were the houses of the courtiers and army officers. Behind the inner wall lived the caliph's relatives and the most important officials. The hub of the city was the caliph's palace. Between the inner and middle walls each of the main streets became lined with all manner of shops, making four central markets. The ordinary people of Baghdad lived outside the walls.

From 'Early Islam' by Desmond Stewart, 1967.

Activities...

1 Using Source A draw your own plan of the city of Baghdad in the 10th century. Compare your diagram with other people's.

2 Source A gives a completely different picture of the city of Baghdad from Sources B and C. Why is this?

3 Why is it so difficult for us to get an accurate picture in our minds about the city of Baghdad under Harun al-Rashid?

Nothing now remains of the Abbasid capital of Baghdad. Because there were no local sources of stone, it was built from clay bricks dried in the sun. Unfortunately brick does not last as well as stone. Invaders flattened much of the city and modern Baghdad is built on the ruins. However, remains of other Abbasid buildings have survived at **Samarra**. This was a city built 80 miles along the Tigris from Baghdad. It was briefly the Abbasid capital from 833 to 893. Samarra has the largest mosque ever built, the **Great Mosque**, with its spiral minaret, or **Malawiya**. Samarra gives us a hint of the glories of Baghdad under the Abbasids.

D

SOURCE

C

SOURCE

An image of the city of Baghdad from a Hollywood film.

The spiral minaret, or Malawiya, at Samarra.

3.5 The Role of Men and Women

The Koran said that men and women should be equal. But it also said that they should have different roles. (See Sources A and B.)

In some ways, the rules of Islam brought few changes and Muslims continued to live as they had before. Women stayed in charge of the home and the children. Men provided food and shelter. Men continued to have more than one wife if they wanted. Arranged marriages were common. This was a system where a marriage was arranged by the families of young Muslims. Usually, they didn't make the choice themselves. This was also common in many other parts of the world. (See Source D.)

But in other ways, Islam improved the lives of women. There had been rules to protect women before. But Muslim men were more likely to follow the rules when they were in the Koran. The Koran said that all women should be protected; that men should behave properly towards them; that they should be respected.

A SOURCE

In Islam women have the same rights to own property and be educated. The Koran requires men and women to behave modestly and decently towards one another. For example, men should always be covered from the navel to the knees. Women should cover their whole bodies except their hands and face.

From 'The Muslim World' by Richard Tames, 1982.

B SOURCE

Women are not subservient to men in Muslim society. The man is responsible for the family's welfare and business outside the home, and the woman controls things inside. But women expect to be treated with respect. They regard themselves as equally important as men; this was made clear in the Koran.

From 'Islam' by Rosalyn Kendrick, 1989.

C SOURCE

The arrangements were started by the mothers. Then a contract was drawn up, stating the girl's age (usually 12–20), and the price that the man paid to his bride, which remained hers even if they were divorced. Should a man and wife argue, they could appeal to a qadi, or judge, who could settle domestic disputes. If the qadi's decision failed to solve the problem, the husband could divorce his wife. He could remarry immediately but his wife had to wait three months. (This was in case she was pregnant.)

From 'Early Islam' by Desmond Stewart, 1967, describing Islamic arrangements as they would have been in about 1300.

D SOURCE

Parents often chose their child's partner. This was partly because parents paid a dowry, or money to start the marriage. It was usual to give the potential husband and wife a chance to meet, and to refuse at least one suggested partner. The idea of marrying for love was seen as foolish. The idea was that a couple should grow fond of each other after marriage.

From 'Skills in History' by P. Shuter, J. Child and D. Taylor, 1989, describing arrangements made by Christians in England in about 1600.

The Koran allowed men to have up to four wives as long as they treated them all equally. Having more than one marriage partner is called **polygamy**. Muslim women could only have one husband. There are many possible reasons for polygamy. Muslims believe that in the Koran, God said that marriage is the religious duty and privilege of **all** women. Allowing men to have more than one wife meant that there would always be enough men for all women to be able to marry. It is interesting that permission for polygamy was revealed to Muhammad just after many Muslim men were killed in the Battle of Uhud. Muslims also say that polygamy means that men are less likely to be unfaithful to their wives, and that this reduces the likelihood of unmarried mothers. They also say that some women welcome the extra help with housework and looking after children, especially if they are ill for a long time.

E
SOURCE

The housework didn't allow a Muslim wife to keep her feminine charms. The old Arab custom of having young wives living with older house-proud ladies was worth keeping. So Muhammad came up with an answer. Muslims might have up to four wives at a time.

From 'The Clash of Cultures' by Brian Catchpole, 1981.

Activities...

1 **a** How did Islam change the role of Muslim men and women?
   b What things stayed much the same?

2 Look at the reasons given in the text for polygamy. Explain them under these two headings:
   a religious reasons,
   b practical reasons.

3 Read Source E. Do you think that a Muslim would be satisfied with this explanation of polygamy? Explain your answer.

4 Are arranged marriages an invention of Islam? What do you think are the advantages and disadvantages of arranged marriages?

F
SOURCE

A qadi listening to a dispute between a man and his wives, (painting dated 1237).

3.6 Religious Life

The religious rules of Islam have remained the same since the death of Muhammad. For example, the key beliefs were, and still are, the '**Five Pillars of Islam**': faith, prayer, charity, fasting and pilgrimage.

The first pillar was faith in Allah and His teaching. All that was needed to become a Muslim was to believe and say, 'There is no god but Allah, and Muhammad is His Prophet'. This chant is called the **shahada** and it is still used at a Muslim's birth, throughout life and at funerals. It is a poetic phrase when spoken in Arabic: 'La ilaha illa Allah; Muhammad rasul Allah'. Muslims also believed that the Koran was the exact words of God. God made the world and would send people to Heaven or Hell when they died. They believed that Jesus was also an important prophet of God, but not his son.

The second pillar, called **salat**, was prayer five times a day. Before each prayer, Muslims washed their face, arms and feet and passed their wet hands over their heads. Muslims were called to prayer at the mosques by **muezzins** shouting from the minarets. Prayers were not led by priests, but by laymen called **imams**. Because the prayers had to be said in the direction of the Ka'ba in Mecca, a decorated arch, or **mihrab**, was always set in the wall of the mosque to show this direction.

A SOURCE

A Muslim's funeral followed a strict ritual which included the wailing of women and readings from the Koran. Washed and wrapped in a seamless white shroud, (dipped on pilgrimage in the waters of Mecca's sacred Zamzam well), the body was laid to rest on its side, facing the holy city.

From 'Early Islam' by Desmond Stewart, 1967.

B SOURCE

A group of Muslim pilgrims from a painting dated 1237.

The next pillar was **zakat**. This said that all Muslims should give part of their income to charity every year. The fourth pillar, called **saum**, was fasting (going without food) during the Muslim month of **Ramadan**. This is when the Koran was first revealed to Muhammad. The final pillar was the **hajj**, the promise to go on a pilgrimage to Mecca at least once. A trip to the Ka'ba had been an Arab tradition before Muhammad and Islam adopted it.

Muslims also made laws based on their religion. These laws are called the **shari'a**. They make up most of the laws of Muslim countries. They are based on the Koran and **Hadith**. Hadith are the wise sayings of Muhammad. They were told over and over again until eventually they were written down.

Muslims also promised to fight for Islam if it was threatened. A holy war to defend Islam is sometimes called a **jihad**, but this also means any other kind of effort for Islam. Muslims were not allowed to eat pork, drink alcohol, gamble or lend money for interest.

C

SOURCE

A Muslim burial. The men are wearing thin black strips of mourning on their heads. The domes in the background are the tops of the tombs of wealthy Muslims (picture dated 1237).

Activities...

1 How would becoming a Muslim change somebody's life?

2 Does Source B give us a picture of **all** pilgrimages?

3 Source C is primary evidence, an Arabic painting dated 1237. Source A is a secondary source from a book written in 1967. What parts of Source A can be:
   a **proven** by Source C?
   b **supported** by Source C?
   c **neither proven nor supported** by Source C? What would you need to prove **all** of Source A to be correct?

4 What is the connection between primary and secondary sources?

3.7 Islamic Medicine

The Arabs were keen to learn from the people they conquered. Caliph Mamun, caliph from 813 to 833, built a **House of Wisdom** in Baghdad. Muslim scholars worked there, translating books about medicine, mathematics and science. They searched for books as far away as India and Africa.

Medicine

At the time of Muhammad, many Arabs believed that illness was caused by the gods. But when they conquered Syria and Persia, they found books with better ideas. These had been written by Ancient Greek scholars, like Galen and Hippocrates. They translated these books into Arabic.

Muslim scholars also went further. Hippocrates had stressed the need to observe the patient very carefully when studying disease. **Rhazes**, a Persian born in 865, used this method. He studied patients with fever and learned to tell the difference between measles and smallpox. He wrote over 100 books on medicine. Another Persian, **Avicenna**, born in 980, wrote the *Canon of Medicine*, a survey of the treatment of all known diseases. It was used by doctors in Europe as a textbook until the 17th century.

Muslim doctors used a variety of **drugs**. Potions were made from animal and plant extracts and chemicals like copper sulphate. In Baghdad, inspectors called to check the quality of the drugs. A chemist caught cheating his customers could be fined or even beaten.

By 850 Baghdad had its own hospital. Soon there were 34 hospitals in the Muslim world, more than in all of Europe. Some hospitals had separate wards for different illnesses and special areas for the insane. There were clinics for outpatients and doctors travelled to the areas outside large towns. From 931 doctors in Baghdad had to pass examinations to get a licence.

A **SOURCE**

Smallpox comes after fever, aching in the back and shivering during sleep. The main symptoms are backache, fever, stinging pains, redness of the cheeks and eyes and a difficulty with breathing. Excitement, nausea and unrest are more pronounced in measles than they are in smallpox, while aching in the back is less severe.

From Rhazes, 'On Smallpox and Measles'. Dated about 900.

A page from the Arabic translation of a book by Dioscorides, a Greek doctor. Detailed records of plants used to make medicines were kept. Dated about 1229.

B **SOURCE**

Activities...

1 a Name three Ancient Greek doctors whose medical books the Arabs used.

b Name three Muslim doctors who took the knowledge in these books and improved it.

2 What do you think the Muslim doctor is doing in Source D?

3 Using **both** the text **and** the sources, find as many things as you can in this unit to support the following statements:

a European medicine was quite backward at this time.

b Islamic medicine was very thorough at this time.

They took me to see a knight who had a boil on his leg and a woman with tuberculosis. I applied a poultice to the leg and the boil began to heal. I ordered a fresh diet for the woman. Then a French doctor came and said, "This man has no idea how to cure these people". He sent for a strong man and an axe. The doctor put the leg on a block of wood and said, "Strike a mighty blow and cut cleanly". The marrow spurted out and the patient died at once. He examined the woman and said, "The devil has got into her brain". He took a razor, removed the brain and rubbed it with salt. The woman died at once.

A Muslim doctor describing European medical treatment during the Crusades. Dated about 1150.

Surgery was also improved. **Abulcasis**, a Muslim born in Spain in 936, translated the ideas of the Greek, Paul of Aegina. Muslim doctors practised his methods and improved them. They operated on eyes to remove cataracts and removed cancers. They used tubes as stomach drains to remove fluids and they could amputate arms and legs. They used opium to make patients sleep when they were in pain.

Traders and soldiers who visited Muslim lands took some of this knowledge back to Europe. Most European scholars read Latin and did not know the books of the Ancient Greeks. The first school of medicine in Europe was set up at Salerno in Italy by soldiers coming home from the Crusades. (The Crusades were battles between the Muslims and Christians.)

A medieval Muslim doctor with a patient.

3.8 Mathematics and Science

On their travels, the Arabs learned a new system of **numbers**. Until then, most people used Roman numbers to count things, (I, II, III, IV, V, etc.). But this was not a good system. The Hindus in India were using a better system (1, 2, 3, 4, 5, etc.). The Arabs copied this. It became so well known that we still use it today. But they didn't just copy, they also developed new theories in algebra and geometry. Better mathematics helped farmers measure the size of a field, traders know the storage area of a ship or builders work out the strength of arches.

Muslim scientists also copied useful ideas. For example, they found out about labour-saving devices like the **windmill** and **wheelbarrows** from the Chinese. This is also where they learned how to make **paper**. But they also discovered things themselves. Trying to make new drugs for doctors, they learned about chemicals. (The word *chemistry* comes from Arabic.) By chance, this showed them how to make steel for swords and dyes for carpetmakers. Also, at this time no one knew how eyes worked. Some people believed that they sent out invisible rays. But **Alhazen**, a Persian scientist, discovered that the eye sees light from the sun reflecting off things around us. This started **optics**, the science of light. Later, it helped people make telescopes and microscopes.

The study of the stars, or **astronomy**, was a favourite science of the Arabs. In the desert, travellers needed the stars for direction at night. Muslims also needed to know the time and the direction of Mecca for their daily prayers. To help them learn more about the stars, caliph Harun al-Rashid had the ideas of Ptolemy, the Ancient Greek scholar, translated into Arabic. Caliph Mamun built an observatory to study the stars at the House of Wisdom. The Muslims also improved the Greek device called the **astrolabe**. This was an instrument which could be used to measure the height and position of the stars and to tell the time.

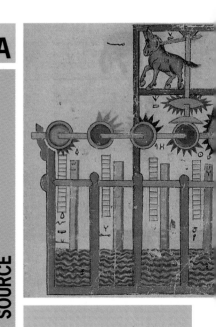

SOURCE **A**

An Arab called Jazari invented this machine in about 1250. Machines like this were used in Iraq. The donkey moved a post which was connected to wheels with gears on them; these wheels lifted four large scoops which can just be seen under the water on the diagram. The scoops rose one at a time, lifting water from the river into canals that watered the fields. This was a big help to farmers.

SOURCE **B**

A picture from a 16th century Muslim manuscript showing astronomers studying the stars.

This is the same simple sum in Roman and Arabic numerals. The Roman numerals are very hard to add up. The Romans had no symbol for zero and you can't separate their numbers into columns of tens and units.

XIII	13
+ *VI*	+ 6
XIX	19

C

An Arab map of the constellation of the Great Bear. How were maps like these useful?

Activities...

1 From the text and sources, make a list of the useful new things the Arabs found out about.

2 Arrange your list from question 1 into ideas which:
   a helped traders, craftsmen and farmers;
   b helped them with their religion;
   c explained mysteries;
   d made their lives more comfortable.

3 Read the section on chemistry again. Do you think the Arabs always knew what use their studies would be?

4 Overall, why do you think the Arabs were so interested in new ideas?

Traders and travellers were also helped by the astrolabe. It could be used with maps of the stars to find exactly where travellers were and the direction they needed to go. The Arabs could now find out about countries thousands of miles away. They visited central Africa with its mysterious animals. The first Arab description of China appeared in 851. Muslims visited Russia in 921. In the 11th century the scientist **Biruni** visited India. His detailed book told the whole story, including joined-together twins he had seen in Siam (hence 'Siamese twins'). Arab geographers drew maps of the world. They became convinced that the world was round.

D

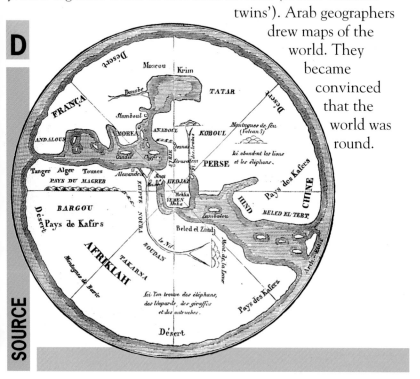

This is a French copy of an old Arab map. How can you tell it was a Muslim map?

3.9 Schools and Universities

Before Muhammad, there were no schools for Arab children. Parents taught their children what they needed for life in the desert. Education was important to Muhammad. His sayings make this clear. Teaching the Koran was vital. The first thing a father taught his children was the shahada. (See page 28.) Another thing was to make sure the Muslims had a strong army. Caliph Umar told Muslims, 'Teach your boys swimming, archery, horse-riding and the appreciation of poetry'.

As soon as the Muslims settled down in the lands they had conquered they started to set up schools. Rich parents had private teachers for their children. But the mosques soon set up schools called **kuttabs**, which charged very low fees. Boys of seven and over would go. Most of the time they chanted or wrote from the Koran. But there was also a little poetry and mathematics. Girls might be sent along for the teaching about Islam but that was probably all.

For the children of the poor, this was as much teaching as they got. But the Arabs needed clerks and administrators, and by about 700 the kuttabs were expanding and taking older children for parents who could afford the fees. The Koran remained the most important part of their education, although mathematics was also important.

A scene from a mosque school in Baghdad in 1237. One boy in the background swings the fan to keep the class cool. Another stands to chant the Koran. The others, all boys, scratch the Koran on to stone tablets.

B **SOURCE**

A scene from the library of a mosque, also dated 1237. Young men listen while one of them reads from a book – not necessarily the Koran. Notice all the books on the shelves.

There was no system of higher education for many years. Only the sons of the very rich continued their studies in their teenage years. They had specially qualified teachers. But there were discussion groups for adults in philosophy, mathematics and poetry at the mosques. The mosques also often had their own libraries which people could use.

Then in 978, in Cairo, Egypt, the al-Azhar mosque was founded. Its school grew into a university. It is perhaps the oldest in the world. It had free tuition, plus board and lodging. Later other Muslim universities were founded at Baghdad, Granada in Spain, and Fez in Morocco. These were all started long before the first chartered university in Christian Europe. That was set up with the help of Muslims at Naples in Italy just before Oxford and Cambridge universities in England.

Every mosque has a school where young Muslims do their Islamic studies. In Britain this usually takes place between 4 and 6 p.m., five nights a week.

    Children in Muslim countries do their Islamic studies in normal school lessons during the day. They are the most important lessons but there are lots of other subjects.

    Boys and girls start Islamic studies aged five. Girls finish at 12; boys go on until they are at least 15.

A description of Muslim education today from 'Islam' by Rosalyn Kendrick, 1989.

Activities...

1 Some of the phrases that follow are causes and some are effects. Put the phrases together to make sentences and underline the phrases that you think are **causes**.
Muslims need to know the rules of Islam...
Because the Koran is the message of God...
Schools started to take older children...
The first university in Christian Europe was founded...
   ..it was the most important part of lessons.
   ..since educated clerks were needed.
   ..because of the example of the Muslims.
   ..so all mosques had schools.

2 Most of this unit is about Muslim schools a thousand years ago. Source D is about Muslim schools today. List some things that have changed. List some things that have stayed the same.

3.10 Trade and Ships

Baghdad was ideally sited for trade. It was on a canal linking the Rivers Tigris and Euphrates and close to the Mediterranean and Red Seas. From about 800 its **bazaars** (market places) were bustling with traders from all over the known world. They bought and sold with the silver **dirham** or the gold **dinar**. Money-changers would swap other coins for these. Later they took written promises to pay which were like cheques (the word comes from the Arabic *sakk*).

Some of the traders went by **land**. Traders going north into Russia and Scandinavia used horses and carts. They took perfume, carpets, grain from the fields around Baghdad and rice from Egypt, and came back with furs, falcons and armour. The Arabs used camels to carry heavy loads over long distances. From about 900, they were crossing the Sahara into central Africa. They took leather, glass and pottery, and came back with black slaves, gold, ostrich feathers and ivory. The long journeys across hot, dry deserts were hard, thirsty and very dangerous. Bandits raided the trading caravans.

Muslim leaders set up strings of small fortresses, called **caravansaries**, in the deserts where traders could rest overnight. Otherwise they slept under the stars before setting off again at a steady three miles per hour on their long journey.

SOURCE A

A market scene in Baghdad in 1237. A Muslim family look at the black slaves on sale. The trader in the background weighs coins to be sure of their value.

SOURCE B

A hoard of silver from a 10th century Viking grave containing Arab coins, found in Sweden.

C

SOURCE

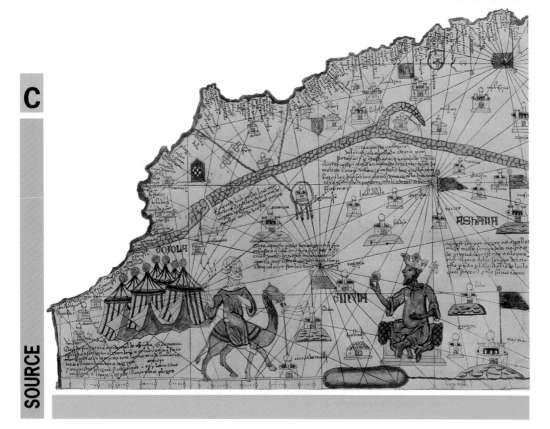

A map of North Africa dated about 1400. It would have been drawn from the accounts of Arab travellers and shows an Arab trader being offered a gold nugget by the King of Mali. Many of the main settlements are shown by mosques.

Other trade went by **sea**. The Arabs had no tradition of sailing but they quickly learned new skills. They sailed across the Mediterranean to Italy and Spain. They also had fast **dhows** which sailed down the Red Sea or the Persian Gulf to the Indian Ocean. They brought back silk, peacocks, paper and porcelain from China and rubies, spices and dyes from India and East Africa.

From about 1200 they went even further, bringing back pepper, nutmeg, cinnamon and cloves from Indonesia and the Philippines. Muslim sailors used the **astrolabe**, borrowed from the Ancient Greeks, to find their position and the magnetic **compass**, discovered in China, for direction. They also invented a new way of arranging the ship's sails. Ships usually had 'square rigging', square sails *across* the ships, which need wind from behind to blow them along. The Muslims developed 'lateen' sails, which were rigged *along* the ships, allowing them to sail into the wind. This made ships easier to manoeuvre and allowed them to sail along rivers to the cities.

There were practically no Europeans trading with Africa and the Far East at this time. Europe depended on the Arabs for all of their goods and knowledge from these far-off places. The voyages of sailors like Christopher Columbus would not have been possible without the instruments and sails which Europe learned about from the Muslims.

Activities...

1 Make a list of all the parts of the world which the Muslim traders visited.

2 Make a list of the goods which they **imported**, or brought back with them.

3 Make a list of the goods which they **exported**, or took out of their lands to sell.

4 Look at the map on page 5 showing where Muslims live today. Also look carefully at Source C. What other export, one which you cannot sell for money, did the Muslim traders take with them? Explain your answer.

5 The coins shown in Source B were buried in a Viking grave in about 950. What can historians learn from this find?

3.11 The End of the Abbasids

The Abbasids ruled the Islamic world from 750. They were the official caliphs until 1258. However, they lost *real* control long before this. First they lost control of the distant provinces. For example, they never gained control of the Muslim rulers of **Spain** and they soon lost control of **Egypt**. Then, even in **Baghdad**, they ended up taking orders from other people.

Events in Spain

Muslim soldiers invaded Spain in 711. Their armies entered France and got to within 200 miles of the English Channel. But in 732 they were defeated at the **Battle of Poitiers**, near Tours, by Charles Martel, king of the Franks. Even so, Muslims ruled parts of Spain until 1492. The Muslims in Spain were known as **Moors**. They were never controlled from Baghdad.

First one Muslim family and then another ruled Spain. A series of important towns grew up. At first, the main one was **Cordoba**. Others were **Toledo**, **Seville** and **Granada**. They were the most splendid towns in Europe at the time. In the 13th century the Moors built the famous **Alhambra Palace** in Granada. In some bedrooms it even had flushing toilets, made possible by diverting a whole river under the palace. Traders from all over Europe came to buy goods from the Moors. It was in Spain that Europeans first gained the knowledge and skills of the Muslim world. Europe learned about Arabic numbers, papermaking, medical knowledge and musical instruments like the guitar. Spain still shows signs of Muslim culture in its buildings, its music and its food.

B SOURCE

In the ninth and tenth centuries, Cordoba was a city of 200,000 houses, 600 mosques and 900 public baths. Its streets were paved and water was piped to the people. Its library had 600,000 books and there were 50 other libraries in the region. Primary schools were common. In agriculture, the Moors introduced new crops, notably figs, dates, rice and cotton. They improved animal rearing and irrigation of the fields. The Moors had the biggest trading fleet in the Mediterranean and expanded the mining, wool and silk industries.

From 'Spain' by Hugh Thomas, 1964.

A SOURCE

Although it is not the most attractive building the Moors left in Spain, this is an interesting one. It was a hotel for traders, built in Granada in about 1350.

Events in Egypt

By 850, the Abbasids were too weak to control their provinces. In 868 **Ibn Tulun**, their governor in Egypt, refused to pay their taxes and began to rule by himself. He had a large Turkish army to keep him in power. After Ibn Tulun died, the **Fatimids** invaded Egypt from North Africa. They were Shi'ites who claimed to be descended from Muhammad's daughter Fatima. They turned the city of **Cairo** into their new capital. The other major town of Fatimid Egypt was **Fustat**, which had half a million people, some living in five storey buildings with running water and sewers. In 1171 the Fatimids were overthrown by a group of Sunni Muslims from eastern Turkey led by Salah ad-Din. In the West we call him **Saladin**. He set up a ruling Turkish family in Egypt known as the **Ayyubids**. They relied upon Turkish slaves to form a huge army which kept them in power. But in 1250 these slaves, known as **Mamlukes**, rebelled. The Mamlukes ruled Egypt until 1517. Through all this upheaval, Egypt prospered. It had huge food surpluses to sell and Cairo was the wealthiest trading city in the Mediterranean in the 12th century. Its famous al-Azhar university is the oldest still existing in the world.

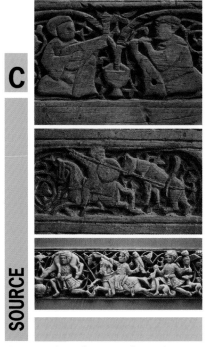

SOURCE C

Carvings from the Fatimid period in Egypt. The top two are wooden panellings from walls: one was in a palace, the other in a hospital. The bottom one was an ivory decoration on furniture.

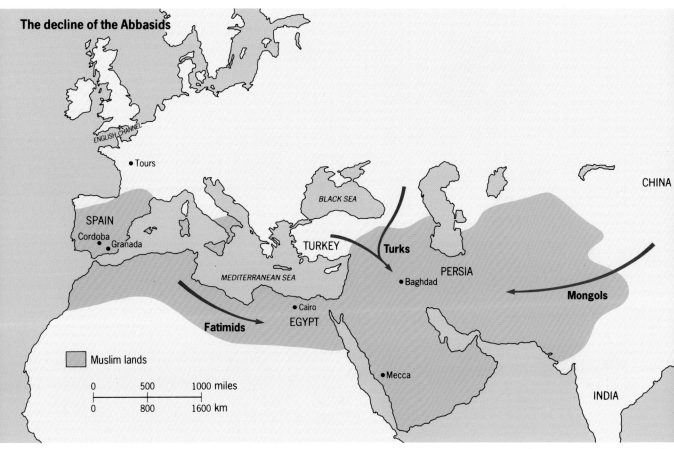

The decline of the Abbasids

ENGLISH CHANNEL

• Tours

SPAIN
Cordoba •
• Granada

BLACK SEA

TURKEY

Turks

PERSIA
• Baghdad

Mongols

MEDITERRANEAN SEA

• Cairo
EGYPT

Fatimids

CHINA

Muslim lands

0   500   1000 miles
0   800   1600 km

• Mecca

INDIA

Events in Baghdad

The Abbasids had taken over control of the Muslim world in 750. But by about 850 the Arab caliphs were chosen by the army and had to do what the soldiers wanted. In 945 a powerful Persian family, called the **Buyids**, took over Baghdad. The Buyids allowed the caliphs to stay, but they had no real power. They were **puppet rulers**, who had to do as they were told. In 1055 new invaders swept through Syria and Persia. They were the **Seljuk Turks**, Muslims from the north, and their leader, Toghrul Beg, captured Baghdad. He allowed the caliphs to stay in Baghdad, but he took the title of **sultan** (ruler), and kept real power to himself. For 200 years the Abbasid caliphs had to do what they were told by the Seljuks. The Arabic and Persian cultures which had shaped the Muslim world were joined by a Turkish influence.

The end of the Abbasids eventually came in 1258. People from central Asia called the **Mongols** invaded the area. They were led by **Ghengis Khan**, but he died before he could attack Baghdad. It was his grandson, Hulagu, who attacked the city. In a six-day siege, he used flamethrowers to overcome the defenders.

Activities...

1 What were the similarities and what were the differences between Moorish Spain and Fatimid Egypt?

2 Here is a list of the groups of people who were in control in Baghdad from 750 to 1258, but they are in the wrong order. Write the list in the right order.
Buyids, Mongols, Abbasids, Seljuk Turks.

3 When do you think the power of the Abbasids came to an end: 850, 945, 1055 or 1258? Compare your answer with other people's. Try to convince them that your answer is the right one.

4 Do you think the painter of Source D and the writer of Source E admired the Mongols or feared them? Explain your answer.

The Abbasids lose control of Muslim lands 750-1258

Muslims conquer Spain	Exiled Umayyad dynasty controls Muslim Spain

711   1031

Abbasid control gradually getting weaker	Tulunite dynasty in control	Fatimid dynasty in control

868   970

The Umayyads rule from Damascus	Abbasid caliphate starts	Army dominates the Abbasid caliphs	The Buyids control the Abbasid caliphs

750   about 830   945   1055

Hulagu leads the Mongol siege of Baghdad in 1258. From a 15th century Persian manuscript.

When at last the city fell, the caliph was kicked to death and half of the city's two million people were slaughtered, including most of the caliph's family. The irrigation system which watered the fields around Baghdad was destroyed. This meant that the huge city could not be fed. The most glorious time in the history of Baghdad was finished. The Abbasid dynasty had ended.

E They came, they uprooted, they burned, they killed, they destroyed, they departed.

A historian from eastern Persia writing about the Mongol invaders in the 13th century.

Various Muslim families control Muslim Spain

Ayyubid dynasty in control	Mamluk dynasty in control

1250

The Seljuk Turks control the Abbasid caliphs	Baghdad destroyed by the Mongols

1258

☐ Events in Spain

☐ Events in Egypt

☐ Events in Baghdad

3.12 The Crusades

For Christians, the area where Christ had lived was called the Holy Land. Bethlehem, Nazareth and Jerusalem were holy places. Ever since the death of Christ, Christians had gone on **pilgrimages**, or journeys there. Some of these holy places are also sacred to Muslims. They believe that Muhammad visited heaven from Jerusalem. The Dome of the Sacred Rock Mosque is there and Jerusalem is the third most holy city in the Muslim world.

The Holy Land was ruled by Christians when Muhammad was alive. After his death, this area was one of the first places the Muslims captured. The Muslim caliphs let the Christian pilgrims carry on visiting the Holy Land.

A

A 14th century French illustration of the Crusaders attacking Jerusalem.

But in 1055, the Seljuk Turks took control in Baghdad. Their sultans did not treat the Christian pilgrims as well. Many were insulted, attacked and even killed. This made the Christians in Europe very angry. In 1095, the leader of the Christian Church, Pope Urban, made an appeal for Christians to recapture the Holy Land. It would be a pilgrimage and a holy war; a war for the cross, or **Crusade**.

The **First Crusade** set out for the Holy Land in 1096. It was made up of about 50,000 knights, mainly from France. The Crusaders had a 2,000 mile journey by land. They were led by noblemen like Robert of Normandy, William the Conqueror's son. Some went for religious reasons, some for adventure or the chance to win riches. In 1099, they arrived outside the walls of Jerusalem. The Muslims (the Crusaders called them Saracens) defended stoutly. It was over a month before the city walls were crossed. Once inside, the Christian soldiers killed every Muslim they could find.

B

The Crusaders used huge wooden catapults to fling rocks at the walls. They built towers on wheels to roll close to the walls. One of the siege towers had a huge wooden statue of Jesus strapped to the front. When they broke through, they killed everyone they could find, men, women and children. To them, they were all unbelievers in God's holy city.

The siege of Jerusalem by the Crusaders. Described in 'Core Skills in History Two' by P. W. Gardner and R. Bateman.

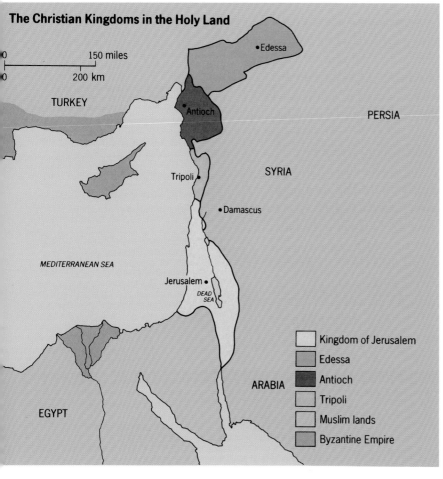

The Christian Kingdoms in the Holy Land

150 miles
200 km

TURKEY

•Edessa

•Antioch

PERSIA

Tripoli•

SYRIA

•Damascus

MEDITERRANEAN SEA

Jerusalem•

DEAD SEA

Kingdom of Jerusalem
Edessa
Antioch
Tripoli
Muslim lands
Byzantine Empire

ARABIA

EGYPT

C **SOURCE**

If you take the right path, you will be forgiven all your sins. This path is to make war on the Infidel (non-believers).

An extract from Pope Urban's speech, according to William of Malmesbury who lived at the time.

D **SOURCE**

Our men entered the city, chasing the Saracens into Solomon's Temple and killing them so that all the Temple was streaming with their blood. Our men rushed round the city seizing gold and silver, horses and all sorts of goods. Then they all came rejoicing to worship at the Church of the Holy Sepulcre. Next morning, they went up to the Temple roof, where many were hiding, and cut off their heads. Many Saracens committed suicide by throwing themselves off the roof.

A medieval Christian manuscript, the 'Gesta Francorum', describing the capture of Jerusalem.

The Crusaders set up Christian kingdoms in the lands they had captured. These were the kingdoms of Jerusalem, Tripoli, Antioch and Edessa. Parts of these kingdoms lasted for almost 200 years. Naturally the Crusaders and Muslims mixed with each other. The Crusaders were amazed by the quality of the Muslim decorations, carpets, furniture and porcelain. For the first time they enjoyed new foods such as apricots, figs, sugar and lemons. They used cool cotton and silk clothes instead of their own hot woollens. They discovered the use of soap and learned better medical treatments. From Muslim buildings, they learned, for example, how to make pointed arches and pillars which could carry great weights. They also learned how to defend castles by using round towers and **machicolations**. These were narrow gaps in the walls which allowed defenders to shoot arrows or drop rocks on attackers. The Muslims had very little to gain from the Crusaders apart from increased trade with Italy and improved weapons and armour.

In 1144 Edessa was recaptured by the Muslims. The **Second Crusade** came from Europe to try to get it back, but failed. Then, in 1187, a new Muslim leader called **Saladin** attacked the Christian kingdoms. First he defeated the Christians at the Battle of Hattin. He ordered all of the Christian soldiers who survived to be put to death. He then recaptured Jerusalem. The Muslim soldiers celebrated. They wanted to kill all of the Christians inside, but he refused to let them. The **Third Crusade** was sent to drive Saladin out of the Holy Land. One of its leaders was Richard I of England, **Richard the Lionheart**. There were several bloody battles, but Saladin's army was too strong. All Richard could do was to make a truce with Saladin in 1192. This allowed the Christians to live in the cities, like Acre, on the Mediterranean coast and visit the holy places. During the next hundred years the Muslims gradually recaptured the Christian cities. Several new crusades were sent to help them, but all failed. In 1291 the last of the Christian cities fell. The Crusades had failed.

A historian called Fulcher of Chartres, who went on the First Crusade and lived for a while in the Kingdom of Jerusalem.

F

SOURCE

A game of chess between a Crusader and a Saracen.

G SOURCE

The gateway to an Arab desert palace, built near Damascus in about 730.

H SOURCE

The gatehouse of Rockingham Castle.

Activities...

1 Finish each of these sentences. In every case the ending is either:

...Christians

or ...Muslims

or ...Christians and Muslims.

a Jerusalem was a holy place for ...
b The Crusaders were ...
c The Seljuk Turks were ...
d In 1099 Jerusalem was captured by ...
e In 1187 Jerusalem was captured by ...

2 Who does this describe: Robert of Normandy, Richard the Lionheart or Saladin?
'He went to the Holy Land to recapture it from the enemy. He captured Jerusalem and let most of the people living there escape to the coast.'
Explain your answer.

3 'Christians went on Crusades to free the Holy Land.' Read the text on page 42 and look at Sources A to D. How far do you agree with this statement?

4 Could a Muslim have said the same as the Pope in Source C? Explain your answer.

5 Look at the castles shown in Sources G and H. What are the similarities?

6 If a Crusader who had lived in the Kingdom of Jerusalem went home to Europe, what could he have taken home or talked about to impress his friends?

4.1 Re-shaping the Muslim World

Unit 3.11 showed how the Abbasids lost control of the Muslim world. Arab control stretching from China to the Atlantic Ocean would never reappear. Instead, the Muslim world was divided up, as different parts were conquered by different invaders. New empires emerged. Some only lasted a few years, but others lasted for centuries. Islam survived all of this. The invaders became Muslims and their empires were Muslim too.

Most of these empires were set up by invasions of people from the east. They were the **Mongol-Tartar** people from the barren wastes of central Asia. They were fierce warriors, nomads who lived in tents and fought on horseback. From about the year 1000 they came sweeping across Asia into the wealthy cities of the Muslim world. At first, they destroyed cities and massacred their people. But as the warriors were joined by settlers, they built up the cities again and created rich new empires.

The Turks were one group of these people. The **Seljuk Turks** captured Baghdad in 1055. The **Ayyubids** and the **Mamlukes** were Turks who captured Egypt. They were the first to take power over the Muslim world from the Arabs and Persians. (See pages 38–39.)

Then the **Mongols** attacked, led by **Ghenghis Khan**. They destroyed Baghdad in 1258 and captured most of the Middle East. Later, a rival Mongol invader appeared in 1369. This was Timur the Lame, sometimes called **Tamerlane**. He ruled an empire based around Samarkand. But Tamerlane's empire did not last long after his death.

In 1502 a new empire grew up in Persia led by Ismail Safavi. This **Safavid** empire lasted until about 1720. Further east, another Mongol, **Babur**, captured most of India and set up an empire which was to last until the 19th century. This is known as the **Mughal Empire**.

However, we are going to look at just one of the new empires. It was an empire started by Turks. It grew up in Asia Minor in about 1300 under the Turkish leader Osman. The empire was named after him and it lasted until about 1920. It was the **Ottoman Empire**. The rest of this book is about the Ottomans.

A SOURCE

The Gur Emir, built by Tamerlane and finished in 1434. It houses his tomb.

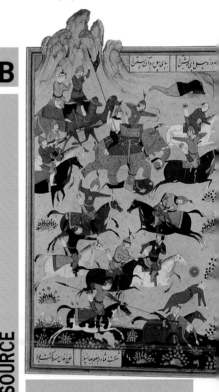

B SOURCE

Miniature painting showing an elephant being used in battle.

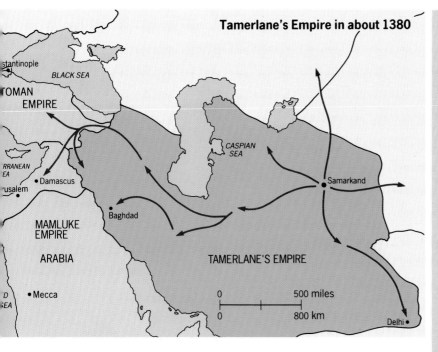

Tamerlane's Empire in about 1380

Tamerlane was born in 1336. He became the ruler of his homeland of Turkestan. His people called him Timur, but he had an illness called gout which gave him a limp and thus he became known as 'Timur the Lame'. In the West, this became Tamerlane. His capital was at Samarkand. From 1369 his armies invaded Russia, India and Persia. He destroyed many cities and murdered their people. It is said that after his capture of Delhi he had the skulls of 80,000 victims piled up outside the city gates. But he was also interested in the arts and he built as many beautiful buildings as he destroyed. Muslim building at this time is famous for the large areas of walls decorated with highly-coloured tiles. (See Source A.)

Ismail Safavi declared himself shah in 1502. The **Safavids** built up a Persian Empire which lasted until about 1720. Shah Abbas (1587–1629) was the greatest of all the Safavid rulers. Under the Safavids, with their capital at Isfahan, the Shi'ite sect became dominant in Iran. It still is. Also at this time Persian artists created the best miniatures in Islamic history. (See Source B.) Miniatures are small paintings used to decorate books.

Babur was a Mongol prince descended from Tamerlane. In 1526 his armies conquered India and set up a new Muslim empire with its capital at Delhi. It is known as the **Mughal Empire**. The fourth Mughal emperor, Shah Jahan, built the most famous Muslim shrine in the world. When his wife died giving birth to their child, he built the Taj Mahal in her memory.

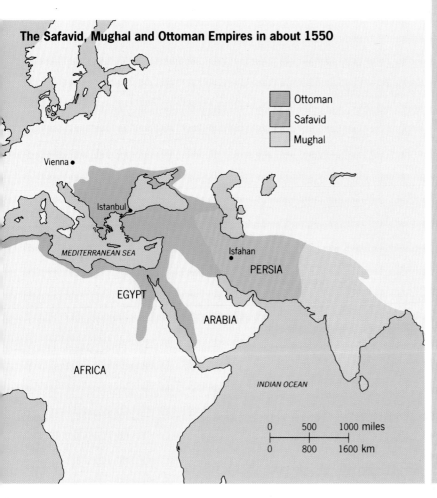

The Safavid, Mughal and Ottoman Empires in about 1550

Ottoman
Safavid
Mughal

4.2 Rise of the Ottoman Empire

In about 1300 a group of Muslim Turks in Anatolia (present-day Turkey) started to attack their neighbours to get more land for themselves. They were led by **Osman** (sometimes known as Othman). They attacked other Turks and also the Christian Byzantine Empire. A series of warlike sultans followed Osman; they became known as the Ottomans. In 1451 **Mehmet II** became the Ottoman sultan. His ambition was to capture **Constantinople**, the capital of the Byzantine Empire.

Mehmet prepared carefully and in 1453, he launched his attack. The siege of Constantinople lasted six weeks. Barbaro, a soldier from Venice who escaped, said that so many defenders were killed that the heads floating in the sea reminded him of melons floating in the canals of Venice. But Mehmet ordered that the buildings should be spared. He renamed the city **Istanbul** and made it his capital. He built new palaces, schools, hospitals and mosques. Istanbul was to become the splendid centre of the world's biggest Muslim empire for 450 years.

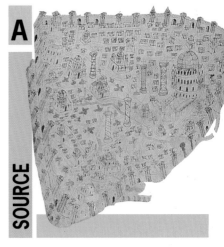

A 15th century map of Constantinople.

A 16th century miniature painting showing Mehmet II leading his troops into Constantinople.

C

Constantinople had the sea on two sides and, on the west, a land wall. Once it had controlled the seas all around the city. But now the Ottomans had built two naval bases in the Bosphorus so that their ships could cut off food supplies. Mehmet II massed his troops on the land side. He had at least 150,000 men and enormous cannons. One took 60 oxen to move and 200 men to hold it on its wagon.

The city had three lines of walls: the inner wall was 40 feet high with towers; a second wall ran parallel to and outside it; the third wall was the stone facing of the foss (ditch) around the city. The defenders massed around the second wall, because the inner wall was in a bad state of repair. They numbered about 7,000 men. A great chain went across the Golden Horn to protect the city harbour.

From 12 April onwards, the Turkish guns bombarded the city walls and the Turkish soldiers tried to fill in the foss. Great gaps appeared in the walls. Mehmet's engineers managed to bring ships overland from the Bosphorus. On 22 April, 70 Turkish ships appeared in the Golden Horn.

Mehmet keyed up his forces for a final assault on 29 May. About an hour after midnight the attack began: first the Bashi-Bazouks, then the Anatolian Turks and finally the janissaries, who eventually gained access to the city.

Extracts from the work of a modern historian writing in 'The Rise of Islam', 1969.

D

Previous sieges failed because the city was supplied by sea. But Mehmet built naval forts, to help his ships. When access for his 125 vessels into the Golden Horn was blocked, the fleet was hauled overland. On land, cannon tore into the city walls; the 7,000 defending troops beat back the Turks. But the cannon breached the walls and they poured through.

From 'Religion at the Crossroads' by J. Milton, R. Steinberg and S. Lewis, 1980.

E

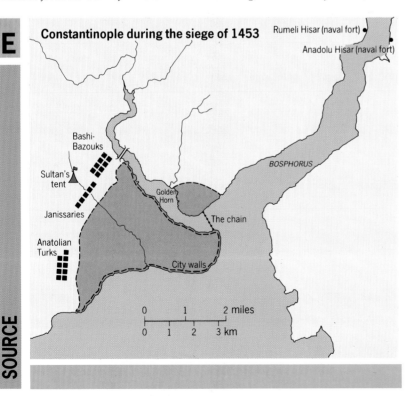

Constantinople during the siege of 1453

Activities...

1 **a** What can you learn from Source B about the methods of attack and defence in warfare at this time?

   b Do you think the attackers or defenders were better off?

2 Source C gives us most information about the siege. Draw a table with two columns. In one column write down a list of things which Source C tells us. In the other column, write down what the other sources tell us which **agrees or disagrees** with Source C.

4.3 Expansion of the Ottoman Empire

The Ottomans used fear to help them expand their empire. (See Source A.) But fear alone was not enough. The cream of the Ottoman army was the **janissaries**. They were Christians, captured as boys, who had converted to Islam and then trained as elite soldiers. They were the sultan's personal slaves, fighting for Allah. They were not allowed to marry or own property, so the army was their life. The janissaries could always be recognized in battle by their white headgear. Originally they were archers, but later they were issued with handguns. No other Muslim army had such advanced weapons. The Ottoman Empire also became a great naval power. It paid the fierce **Barbary pirates** from North Africa to fight for the empire. They terrorized the southern coasts of Europe and dominated the Mediterranean. Their leader, Barbarossa, became the admiral of the Turkish fleet. His ships were more mobile than those used in Europe. He brought back to Istanbul treasure and riches plundered from the ports and ships of the West.

A **SOURCE**

Murad I combined military brilliance with brutality. Capturing Chorlu, halfway between Adrianople and Constantinople, he ordered the garrison to be massacred and its commander beheaded. This so terrified the people of Adrianople that they gave up the city without a fight.

From 'Religion at the Crossroads' by J. Milton, R. Steinberg and S. Lewis, 1980.

At first the Ottomans used this military might to attack Europe. After Constantinople, **Mehmet II** conquered Athens and the Greek peninsula, Albania, the area around the Black Sea and the whole of Anatolia. By 1477 he had captured Bosnia and was on the verge of capturing Italy. The Christian European states rarely got together to oppose the Muslims. But Mehmet died in 1481 and the Ottomans became involved in wars against the Safavids.

The Safavids were Shi'ite Muslims from Persia. They had tried to convert Muslims to the Shi'ite sect all across the Middle East. The Ottomans were orthodox Sunni Muslims. Sultan **Selim I** (1512–20) declared a holy war against the Safavids. He drove them back into Persia and captured Iraq and Syria. Victories here were easier than in Europe. His armies swept on to capture Egypt from the Mamlukes. Within eight years, Selim doubled the size of the Ottoman Empire.

B **SOURCE**

Suleiman the Magnificent and his army defeating the Hungarians at the Battle of Mohács in 1526. Notice the white plumed headgear of the janissaries.

C

SOURCE

An Ottoman galley used Christian slaves chained to the oars, and also had sails.

Activities...

1 Copy the map on this page. Mark the areas captured after 1453 by:
   a Mehmet II,
   b Selim I,
   c Suleiman the Magnificent.

2 From the point of view of the Ottomans, which of these sultans made the most important gains after 1453?

3 Why were the Ottomans so successful in battle?

4 Why did the Ottomans fail to capture more of Europe by 1566?

But the greatest Ottoman sultan was still to come. Selim's son, **Suleiman**, became sultan in 1520. He captured Belgrade in 1521, Rhodes in 1522, then the whole of the north coast of Africa. In 1529 Suleiman seemed set to capture Vienna in the heart of Europe. But bad weather reduced the food for his men and horses and made the roads impassable for his cannon. He turned back and again Europe was spared. The map on this page shows how the Ottomans towered over the western world by the time of Suleiman's death in 1566.

The growth of the Ottoman Empire up to 1566

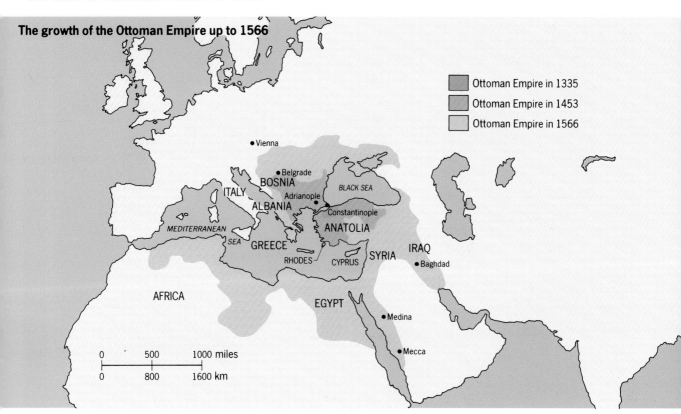

Ottoman Empire in 1335
Ottoman Empire in 1453
Ottoman Empire in 1566

4.4 Life at the Ottoman Court

The sultan lived a life of luxury. Most of the court officials were his personal slaves. His gardeners would fill the grounds of the palace with fine flowers, rare birds and wild animals. For amusement he would go hawking or call for his slave wrestlers, jugglers and dancers. The sultan also had a **harem**. The women of the harem were slaves selected for their beauty and brains. No men entered the harem apart from the sultan, his sons and the black eunuchs who acted as guards. None of the women was ever allowed to leave the harem.

But the sultan also had the business of government to attend to. His power was total but he had advisers. His most important official was the **grand vizier**, and his council of advisers was the **divan**. Suleiman the Magnificent's divan would meet every morning as a court, to hear complaints against people and pass judgment. In the afternoon it would meet to discuss government policy. Each of the advisers had hundreds of officials and clerks to help him collect taxes and apply the laws. All of these officials, from the grand vizier down, were slaves. They were educated in the palace schools and were totally loyal to the sultan.

SOURCE A

The slave who dressed Suleiman put 20 gold ducats in the pockets of his master's silk caftan every morning and was rewarded with the robe and the remaining coins at night.

From 'Religion at the Crossroads' by J. Milton, R. Steinberg, and S. Lewis, 1980.

A miniature painting showing the sultan visiting his harem.

SOURCE B

C

SOURCE

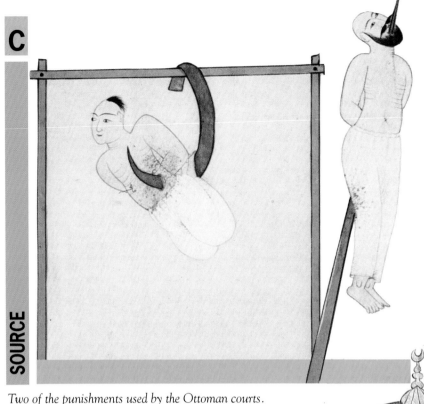

Two of the punishments used by the Ottoman courts.

Activities...

1 List the jobs which were done in and around the court by the sultan's slaves.

2 The Ottomans used very harsh punishments. What do you think of each of the following explanations for this?
  a They used harsh punishments because they believed they were fair.
  b They relied on harsh punishments to make people too frightened to break the law.
  c They were cruel and knew no better.

Away from the capital, there was a network of judges, called **qadis**. These were **ulema**, respected Muslims who had studied the laws of Islam. The Koran was their guide. No one could be punished without their permission, although non-Muslims were tried and punished by their own leaders. Ottoman punishments were very harsh; amputation of a hand for horse stealing, for example. But the Koran allowed harsh punishments. The law was harsh in other parts of the world at that time too. In England, Elizabeth I was on the throne and English punishments were just as severe. The Ottomans had no police force to keep order, they had to rely on fear.

D

SOURCE

The grand vizier chairs a meeting of the sultan's council. The sultan can be seen observing from behind the window at the back.

4.5 Life in the Ottoman Empire

Trade was an important part of the Ottoman Empire. Every city had its **bedestan**, or bazaar. This was the market place where goods from all over the world were bought and sold. The people of the cities depended on the traders for their food and other goods. In Mehmet II's reign the bedestan in Istanbul had over 1,000 stalls. Buyers would haggle over prices. This is still the custom in the market places of the Muslim world. The Ottomans copied the Arab **caravansaries** along the overland trade routes. Caravansaries were fortified stopping places for traders. The sultans wanted to encourage trade so they allowed free food and lodgings for three days to all traders. One great caravansary contained 200 rooms and a courtyard big enough for 5,000 horses.

The bedestan in Istanbul in about 1600.

The profits of trade made the traders wealthy. But they weren't the only ones to benefit. Muslims give some of their income to charity every year. Hospitals often grew up around the bedestan, funded by gifts. The sultans also charged the traders taxes. Mehmet II needed taxes to build up his new capital of Istanbul. He encouraged skilled craftsmen to settle in the city, promising them safety and lower taxes. The Venetian painter Bellini spent a year in Istanbul. The palace schools also produced artists, poets and architects. Many of these craftsmen were used to convert the Christian churches of Constantinople into mosques. Their changes were sometimes simple, but often they added splendid decoration.

Outside the palace, there were also **medreses**, or free schools, for Muslim boys. Suleiman paid for many of these out of income from taxes. Each school was attached to a mosque and taught the ideas of Islam, grammar, geometry and astronomy. Colleges taught the more gifted students when they were older. This was the time of the Renaissance in Europe, when learning and art flourished. But no European capital could match the thriving city of Istanbul for learning and culture.

C

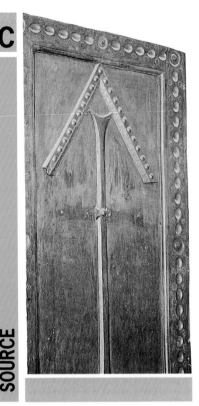

SOURCE

The Hagia Sophia was a splendid Christian church in Constantinople when the Turks captured it in 1453. The Ottomans converted it to a mosque. This is one of the panels altered by the Muslim craftsmen.

B

SOURCE

The mosque of Selim II, built in Konya, Turkey in 1575.

Activities...

1 Explain the change which has been made to the wooden panel shown in Source C.

2 What were:
   a bedestans,
   b caravansaries,
   c medreses?

3 Use the text to find out three reasons why trade was important to the Ottoman Empire. Explain each one and refer to Sources A and B in your answers.

4.6 Decline of the Ottoman Empire

The early Ottoman sultans were talented generals and rulers. From the end of Suleiman's reign the sultans were less able.

Suleiman had broken with custom and taken as one of his four legal wives **Roxelana**, a Russian slave girl from the harem. She convinced Suleiman that his oldest son was plotting to overthrow him. Suleiman ordered him to be strangled. So it was Roxelana's son, **Selim II**, who became the next sultan, in 1566. He was short and fat, had no training or liking for government or war, and drank so much that he was known as **Selim the Sot**. He relied totally on his grand vizier.

Selim knew that the island of Cyprus was famed for its wine. In 1571 he ordered his grand vizier to capture it. But a huge fleet of ships from Europe gathered to defend the island. The ships met at the **Battle of Lepanto**. The Ottomans suffered their first major defeat.

B

SOURCE

Without the constant booty, the soldiers became restless. Many settled down lazily. Even the janissaries were prone to revolt if they were kept idle too long. So they were allowed to marry and take up trades. They stopped being elite troops.

Most of Suleiman's successors were incompetent. Because the sultan was so important a figure in the Ottoman system, this was disastrous. Ottoman methods of farming and industry also became outdated and this was a poor basis for the economy.

A modern historian writing in 'The Rise of Islam', 1969.

A

SOURCE

A painting of Suleiman painted in Europe in the 16th century by Hans Eworth.

By this time the Ottoman Empire had expanded as far as it could. The army could only fight in the spring and summer. By the time it got to the borders of the empire it was too late for a long campaign against new cities. So the conquests stopped.

In 1574 Selim II, drunk on Cyprus wine, slipped in a bath and cracked his skull. Over the next 140 years, thirteen sultans followed. None had the ability of the first Ottoman sultans. Many of them were overthrown in plots. When Mehmet III came to the throne in 1595 he took no chances. He murdered all nineteen of his brothers. Everyone feared for their life. It was impossible to rule under these conditions.

The Ottoman Empire lasted for 350 years like this. It was still huge, with a population of 30 million, but it was weak. It became known as 'The Sick Man of Europe'. It was bullied by other countries and its provinces ignored the orders of the sultans. The last Ottoman sultan was deposed in 1922.

C

SOURCE

The sultans so completely lacked the strong, warlike, dedicated spirit of the first sultans that some historians have doubted whether Selim II really was Suleiman's son. Many of them were cowards, at least one was an imbecile, others were corrupt. Only a few able grand viziers saved the empire.

The janissaries took power into their own hands. They conspired to get the throne for their favourite prince – and then charged him huge sums for their support. They opened their ranks for other Muslims to enrol as janissaries, without the training. The system of the most able slaves getting the best positions in government ended. People started to buy jobs with bribes.

Government funds declined as trade declined and fewer conquests meant less plunder.

From 'Religion at the Crossroads' by J. Milton, R. Steinberg and S. Lewis, 1980.

Activities...

1 **a** What impression do you get of Selim II from Source D?
   b What impression of Suleiman do you get from Source A?
   c Do you think you can trust these impressions?

2 Source C says that some historians doubt that Selim II was really the son of Suleiman. What evidence is there in this unit for thinking this? Do you think that the evidence is strong?

3 Compare Sources B and C. They both give reasons why the Ottoman Empire became weak. What does each source say about:
   a the sultans,
   b the janissaries,
   c government finances?

A 16th century painting of Selim II.

D

SOURCE

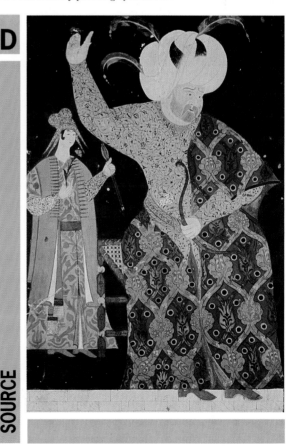

5.1 Architecture

The Arabs learned about building from others. They adopted domes and pillars from the Roman and Greek styles of the Byzantine Empire. They took the pointed arch from the Persians. But **minarets** (the tall towers seen on mosques) were developed by the Arabs themselves. Their main efforts went into religious buildings, like mosques and mausoleums (tombs). But they also built schools, universities and fortresses which still survive.

The Arabs developed a clear style in their buildings. They set the pattern for other Muslim architects all over the world. They also learned design and engineering skills so they could build large buildings. Builders in Europe copied these when building their castles and cathedrals.

B

SOURCE

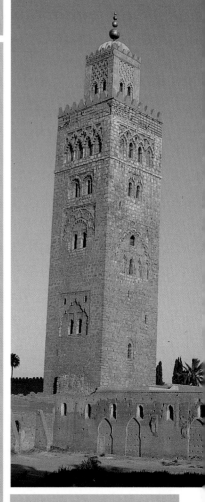

The minaret of the Koutoubia Mosque at Marrakesh in Morocco. Built in the 12th century by the Arabs.

A

SOURCE

The prayer room of the Great Mosque at Kairouan in Tunisia. This mosque was built by the Arabs in the 7th century.

C

SOURCE

Mosques need not be covered. Worship can take place in open courtyards. Every mosque will have somewhere for worshippers to wash before prayer. There are no pews or benches inside. Everyone prays on the floor, which is usually covered by carpet. There are no pictures or statues inside. This is to avoid any hint of idol worship. A domed roof represents the universe and the minaret allows the muezzin to climb up and call Muslims to prayer.

From 'Islamic Worship' by R. Bruce, 1985.

SOURCE

The Blue Mosque, started in 1609 by the Muslim Ottoman Turks, in Constantinople.

F

SOURCE

Regents Park Mosque.

E

SOURCE

The Taj Mahal at Agra in India. Built in about 1635 by the Muslim Mughal ruler Shah Jahan as a mausoleum for his favourite wife who died in childbirth.

Activities...

1 Sources A–F cover about 900 years of Muslim building, starting with the Arabs.
  a What things seem to have remained unchanged?
  b What has changed?

2 a Read Source C. How many features of mosques does it mention which you can see in the other sources?
  b Source C was written about modern mosques. Why does it fit the older ones too?

3 What can buildings tell us about the people who built them?

5.2 The Impact of Islam (2)

The rise of Islam has left its mark on the world.

From about 700, the Muslims gathered the knowledge of the Ancient Greeks from old books. They also learned from China and India. It was only after about 1300 that Europe became interested in all this knowledge. Many of the Greek books had disappeared for ever by then. But the knowledge was not lost. Source A shows how Europe learned from the Muslims.

The Muslims also made a more obvious mark on Europe. Islands like Rhodes, Cyprus, and Sicily were all occupied by the Arabs for a while. A large part of Spain was Muslim for over 700 years. The buildings, the language, the food and the music of these places still show Muslim influence. The Muslim traders also spread their religion outside Europe and the Middle East. Indonesia, in the Far East, has a Muslim population of almost 150 million people today.

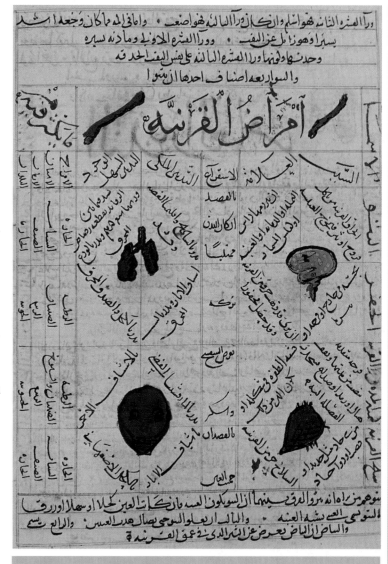

A

SOURCE

A page from the 'Canon of Medicine', written by the Persian doctor Avicenna in 1000. Doctors in Europe used this book until about 1800.

But the biggest impact was on people's lives inside the Muslim world. This huge area was not only united by Islam the religion; it was also united by Islamic society and culture.

The **religious unity** meant that all over this area the Five Pillars of Islam became the centre of people's lives. The belief in one God, daily prayers, acts of charity, fasting and pilgrimages were all shared by millions of Muslims. The Koran was the same in Tunisia as it was in India.

But Islam is not just a religion; it is a way of life. So the whole of **society** changed. Islam had rules about the food people could eat, the way they should dress, the role of women. Islam insisted on fair treatment for all races and all religions. Christians and Jews, for example, were normally treated well. Not all cultures have been so tolerant. Polygamy was strengthened. Gambling and charging interest for lending money were frowned upon. Alcoholic drinks were banned.

People's **culture** changed too. More people lived in towns. Cities grew up where villages had been before. They had mosques with open courtyards, minarets, arches and domes. Their other buildings copied some of these features. Fountains and gardens became more common. Art also changed. The Muslims used tiles for decoration more than any other society. And everywhere Arabic, the language of the Koran, became the common language.

By 1550 this was the Islamic civilization. Today, the lives of the world's 1,100,000,000 Muslims still show the impact of the changes made then.

B SOURCE

A Muslim funeral in modern Spain.

C SOURCE

Muslims outside a mosque in modern Morocco.

Activities...

1 'Europe learned from the Muslims.' Explain this statement with reference to Source A.

2 What kinds of things can you see in Sources B and C which are typical features of Islamic civilization?

3 Life in the Islamic world was different from life elsewhere. Make a list of things which were typical of life in the Muslim world. Here are two to get you started:
   • washing before prayer,
   • a minaret.

4 Look at your list.
   a The Prophet Muhammad has probably got something to do with everything on your list. Explain how.
   b What does this tell you about Islamic society?

5.3 The Challenge for Islam Today

By 1600 the Ottoman Turks were weak. Other countries took over parts of their Muslim empire. By 1900 Britain, France and Italy ruled most of north Africa. At the end of the First World War in 1918 the Turks were punished for supporting Germany. Britain and France took over all of the Arab lands still in the Ottoman Empire. It has only been in the last 40 years that these lands have been allowed to rule themselves again with their own Muslim governments.

Oil has made some Arab countries very rich and powerful since the early 1970s. Some Muslims want to use their wealth to become more like people in the West. People in Europe and the USA enjoy a high standard of living. But other Muslims don't trust the West. They see western culture as evil, where gambling, alcohol and sexual freedom are allowed. Some countries, like Turkey, have relaxed Islamic rules and have become very westernized. But others, like Saudi Arabia and Iran, want to get back to the strict basics of Islam. Their rules on alcohol and punishment, for example, are very rigid.

A

SOURCE

What I refuse to do is abandon Islamic principles. We do not cut off the hand of any who steal to eat. Anyone under such necessity is not to blame. Only he who steals for stealing's sake is open to this penalty. Take another case, adultery. There is no question of stoning the adulterer or adulteress as has been falsely claimed. The punishment is flogging, 100 lashes.

Colonel Gadafi, leader of Libya, quoted by M. Bianco, 'Gadafi, Voice of the Desert', 1975.

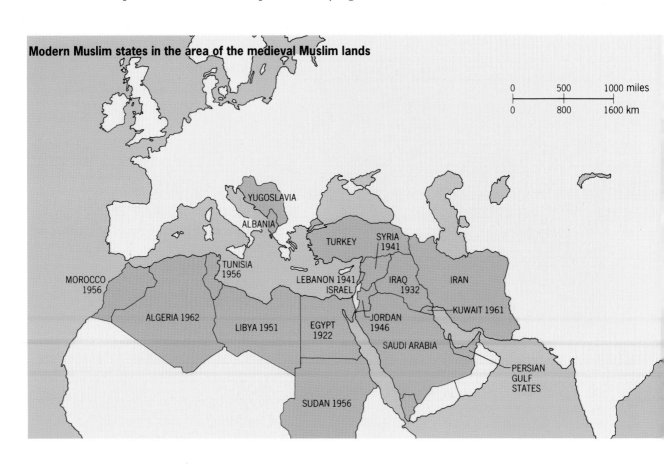

Modern Muslim states in the area of the medieval Muslim lands

0   500   1000 miles
0   800   1600 km

YUGOSLAVIA
ALBANIA
TURKEY
SYRIA 1941
TUNISIA 1956
LEBANON 1941
ISRAEL
IRAQ 1932
IRAN
MOROCCO 1956
KUWAIT 1961
ALGERIA 1962
LIBYA 1951
EGYPT 1922
JORDAN 1946
SAUDI ARABIA
PERSIAN GULF STATES
SUDAN 1956

This has caused tensions. Muslims argue with other Muslims about what they should do. The split between Sunni and Shi'ite Muslims continues. Some Muslims living in non-Muslim countries demand different schools or different food. The people around them often don't understand. This causes confusion and sometimes anger and violence. There have also been tensions between Muslim and non-Muslim countries.

Muslims have a glorious past. Creating a place for Islam in the modern world sometimes causes problems. This makes it vital that the world understands Islam. We hope this book has helped.

B

An illustration from a Muslim book, 'Islam, Beliefs and Teachings', by the Muslim Educational Trust, 1984.

C

Muslim children in an Islamic school in Nelson, Lancashire.

D

Muslim women in the modern world: one solution for a young doctor in South Yemen!

Activities...

1 Compare the map in this unit with the one on page 12. What are the differences between the Muslim areas around the Mediterranean today compared with those in 750?

2 What differences exist today:
   a between the West and Muslim countries?
   b between different Muslim countries?

3 Some Muslim countries are relaxing the rules of Islam to adopt western ways. Others are applying the original rules of Islam. Write two letters to a friend, one persuading him or her that the first way is right, one that the second way is right.